Meaning in Landscape Architecture & Gardens

Meaning in Landscape Architecture & Gardens

FOUR ESSAYS
FOUR COMMENTARIES

Essays by:

Jane Gillette

Susan Herrington

Laurie Olin

Marc Treib

EDITED BY MARC TREIB

LONDON AND NEW YORK

First published 2011 by Routledge,
2 Park Square, Milton Park, Abingdon, Oxon OX14 4RN

Simultaneously published in the USA and Canada by Routledge,
711 Third Avenue, New York, NY 10017

Routledge is an imprint of the Taylor & Francis Group, an informa business

© copyright 2011 Marc Treib, selection and editorial material;
individual chapters, the contributors

The right of the editor to be identified as the author of the editorial
material, and of the authors for their individual chapters, has been
asserted in accordance with sections 77 and 78 of the Copyright,
Designs and Patents Act 1988.

Designed by Marc Treib
Typeset in Century Old Style, Bell Gothic, and Syntax
Printed and bound in Great Britain by
TJ International Ltd., Padstow, Cornwall

*All rights reserved. No part of this book may be reprinted or reproduced or
utilized in any form or by any electronic, mechanical, or other means, now
known or hereafter invented, including photo-copying and recording, or in
any information storage or retrieval system, without permission in writing
from the publishers.*

British Library Cataloguing in Publication Data
A catalogue record for this book is available from the British Library

Library of Congress Cataloging-in-Publication Data
Meaning in landscape architecture / [edited by] Marc Treib.
p. cm.
Includes bibliographical references and index.
1. Landscape design. 2. Landscapes—Psychological aspects.
I. Treib, Marc.
SB472.45.M43 2011
712'.2—dc22
2010041746

ISBN 13: 978-0-415-61725-3 (pbk)
ISBN 13: 978-0-203-82789-5 (ebk)

For Alan Colquhoun

Architect, Thinker,
Educator, Friend

CONTENTS

Marc Treib

Meaning and Meanings: An Introduction *viii*

Laurie Olin

1. Form, Meaning, and Expression in Landscape Architecture *22*

1a. Commentary 1: **What Did I Mean Then or Now?** *72*

Marc Treib

2. Must Landscapes Mean? Approaches to Significance in Recent Landscape Architecture *82*

2a. Commentary 2: **Must Landscapes Mean? Revisited** *126*

Jane Gillette

3. Can Gardens Mean? *134*

3a. Commentary 3: *166*

Susan Herrington

4. Gardens Can Mean *174*

4a. Commentary 4: **Meaning and Criticism** *206*

Bibliography *214*

Contributors *222*

Index *223*

GUSTAFSON PORTER,
PRINCESS DIANA
MEMORIAL FOUNTAIN,
LONDON, ENGLAND,
2004.
[MARC TREIB]

Meaning and Meanings:

An Introduction

Marc Treib

Meaning in Architecture, the pioneering study on the subject of building and significance, first appeared in 1969, with an American edition following one year later.[1] Co-edited by Charles Jencks and George Baird, the book employed a provocative format: in addition to their individual essays each of the authors critiqued the writings of their fellow contributors, with their comments in small type set in the margins, like classical literary annotations. There followed a plethora of articles on the subject which a decade later had come to center on discussions of typology. By the end of the 1970s a lull had set in, perhaps from exhaustion, perhaps from a realization of the inherent limits of the pursuit. The currency of significance in general—and significance in architecture in particular—returned by the mid-1980s when meaning, symbolism, and communication became hot topics for theoretical investigation—with pronouncements tied to postmodern architecture's re-examination of the past.

This involvement with architectural semiotics—the study of signs—followed closely upon the heels of a prevailing interest in structuralism, one of the many theories from beyond the architectural arena commandeered for service within architectural thought, if rarely influential in normal practice. A prime example of this approach was found in the book *Folk Housing in Middle Virginia*, written by the anthropologist and folklorist Henry Glassie, which minutely classified room/cell types in these rural domestic structures without much discussion about the function of these spaces, who built them, and who lived in them.[2] In the eyes of architectural semioticians structuralism fell short as a means by which to talk about the world: it categorized and established relationships—often relying on the grid or the matrix—but it did not address the cultural, social, and significatory aspects of building. My own critique of structuralism is neatly expressed by Dylan Thomas in his poem *A Child's Christmas in Wales*.[3] In recounting the many gifts that were given at the Yuletide of his childhood Thomas cited "books about the wasp that told me everything about the wasp, except why." That "why" was the province of meaning and semiotics, and those interests furthered the basic process of classification that was so much a part of structuralist practice. As it happens, semiotics too ran its course—as trends in architectural theory tend to do, rather neatly on three-year cycles. Semiotics itself was taken to task by poststructuralist thinkers with differing perspectives—based on gender, political stance, postcolonial standpoint, or sexual orientation—bringing us then to deconstruction, neopragmatism, and so on.

Landscape architecture seemed little interested in the subject of meaning other than as applied to intention or display. Estate designers at the turn of the twentieth century looked to historical models, of course, and one could say that meaning is always an implicit aspect of any choice of style. The modernists in turn denied the historical styles—and presumably meaning with them—instead grounding their work in discussions of function and zeitgeist. In the late 1960s, at the very same time that architecture was fumbling around for a theoretical base—borrowing at one time or another from such fields as anthropology, sociology, operational research, behavioral psychology, and of course, literary criticism—landscape architecture discovered ecology and embraced it with a vengeance. The appearance of Ian McHarg's *Design with Nature* in 1969 sealed the deal and to some degree also doomed the design-conscious aspects of landscape practice for decades to come.[4] But, the theory—should we accept it as such—argued in McHarg's classic study was drawn from within the true province of landscape architecture, unlike architecture which continued—and continues—to appropriate and apply external sources to its own would-be theories.

As several of the essays published in this book note, discussions of meaning in landscape architecture held little interest well into the 1980s.[5] True, art historians who used landscape as a subject researched and discussed the iconography of statuary, the imagery and depiction of labor in landscape painting, and the transference of geographical subjects into rendered depictions. But these were academic studies divorced even from the main body of landscape architecture history, and they hardly informed the workings of the profession on an everyday basis. It would be more than a decade of ecology-over-everything before significance became an active topic of discussion.

Perhaps the first true investigation of significance in landscape architecture in the last half century was *The Meaning of Gardens: Idea, Place, and Action*, edited by Mark Francis and Randolph T. Hester, Jr., published in 1990.[6] The book derived from a symposium held the previous year at the University of California, Davis, which drew upon the contributions of participants from a wide variety of fields. Faced with a collection of revised papers with differing approaches, subjects, and scales, the editors wisely grouped them *post priori* into the headings Faith, Power, Ordering, Cultural Expression, Personal Expression, and Healing—a classification system sufficiently broad to have remained valid until today.

At about the same time Anne Whiston Spirn guest-edited an issue of *Landscape Journal* on the subject of "Nature, Form, and Meaning." In her editorial Spirn asked, "Where do landscape forms come from, both those of the natural and cultural landscape? How can those forms be employed in the design of landscape? What sorts of meanings do these forms embody and how do these meanings come to stand for the views and values of a group or a society as a whole?"[7] One of the principal contributors to that issue was Laurie Olin, whose essay "Form, Meaning, and Expression in Landscape Architecture" squarely addressed her questions. Olin, an educator as well as landscape practitioner, began his text with the following sentence:

> *Historically, landscape design has derived a considerable amount of social value and artistic strength from three aspects of the endeavor: the richness of the medium in sensual and phenomenological terms; the thematic content concerning the relationship of society and individuals to nature; and the fact that nature is the great metaphor underlying all art.*[8]

In the pages that followed he examined each of these areas in detail, cautioning that:

> *By adopting strategies borrowed directly from other fields and by referring to work that is itself an abstraction from the referent, many contemporary landscape designers are producing work that is thin, at best a second- or third-hand emotional or artistic encounter.*[9]

Consider that Olin was writing at a time when the concern for ecology and process—and ecology and process alone—was paramount, with nary a breath of meaning in the air. He followed with a discussion of meaning, its derivation and interpretation, citing the architectural theorist Alan Colquhoun's proposal of "natural" or "evolutionary" as opposed to "synthetic" or "invented" meanings. The first group comprises those social beliefs "as a reflection or expression for survival and social perpetuation."[10] It is the synthetic meanings that most pertain to landscape architecture as a creative practice. Olin's interest was rare at that moment, and few writings followed in its wake.

My own interest in meaning in landscape, as I note at the start of "Must Landscape Mean? Approaches to Significance in Recent Landscape Architecture" (published in 1995), derived from my observations of practitioners and students, each trying to validate their design efforts by reference to significance.[11] My skepticism led to an extended investigation, further fueled by the comments of the anonymous reviewers for *Landscape Journal*, who included the late Margaret McAvin and then-editor Robert Riley. Responding to their justified criticism of my original submittal greatly enriched the analysis and the subtlety of the descriptions. Or so I hope.

What remains for me essential, as I noted in my essay, is that meaning does not reside within the object or landscape, that it instead results from a transaction between people and the landscape that serves as a sort of stimulus or catalyst for the transaction. What the designer intends in the design may or may not be manifest, appreciated, or understood by those experiencing the place. What they gather will derive from the cultural matrix in which they have lived paired with their personal experience, knowledge, and feelings. Meaning is ultimately personal, I contend, conditioned by a cultural and temporal frame. To stress that belief, in teaching I continually reminded students of the asymmetrical nature of the transaction between designer and audience, and that the practitioner should always keep in mind the resulting difference between "the intended perception and the perceived intention."

Jane Gillette's contribution, "Can Gardens Mean?" (published in 2003), followed a track in some ways tangential to the two that preceded her.[12] Given a background in literary history, Gillette looked at landscape meaning as a subject in both fiction and physical design. In fiction, she contends, the garden is used symbolically; it is a construct whose sole function is to provide setting and to signal significance. The primary role of the physical landscape, in contrast, is to provide what she terms the "actual." Yes, we may be interested in the iconographic program behind the imagery and structures of a great garden like Stourhead, but this is neither the aspect that holds our attention nor what grants the garden its greatness. It is the experience on site that rules, and as a result Gillette questions the ability of any landscape designer to invest meaning into the place—and in some ways even questions whether meaning can collect over time. Or, as she writes, the "meaningful" garden may be at most a one-liner; it may announce but does not develop an idea. As it happens Jane Gillette and I differ on that particular conclusion. I would counter that Stourhead has accrued heaps of meaning over the centuries and that it today means more than it did in the time of Henry Hoare, its principal maker. It is now an important illustration of British class, political, aesthetic, and preservation history as well as a key work— even a monument—of the world's landscape architectural heritage. But time is required, as are the people who construct that significance.

Some years later, in 2007, Susan Herrington reversed the title of her predecessor's essay by asserting that "Gardens Can Mean."[13] In some ways bypassing Jane Gillette's stance, in some ways confronting it, Herrington returned to the garden itself—transforming Gillette's distinction between cognitive and sensory experience by conflating them, at least to the degree that experience becomes a key part of cognition. "The movement of our bodies, sensations, and emotions," Herrington wrote, "are part of meaning." She has reinforced this position in her commentary, emphatically noting that "impressions and feelings are a part of meaning."

Personally, I would suggest that although sensory experience, as one type of precondition, might normally lead to cognition it need not do so by definition. Perception differs from cognition, from interpretation, and from the production of significance—although they are obviously intertwined and bear on one another. We have all appreciated a tune without thinking about what it means or thinking about it at all. We have all experienced driving for several minutes only to realize that our mind has wandered and that we have little recollection of our thoughts or actions during the period just past. Obviously, our bodies have been aware when our mind has not. It would seem that we can experience while being aware and focused and touched by thought, but equally so when we are literally mindless and interacting with the world through the body alone. Still, the relation of these aspects of thinking and feeling constitutes in itself a thorny subject that might generate yet another round of essays. So let us leave it there, agreeing to disagree.

Then there is the question of how things are done and what forms result. Herrington cleverly rearranges the positions of the stones at Ryoan-ji to demonstrate that the resulting landscape will produce or possess a different meaning. I would probably question that assumption, allowing that the garden would certainly *appear* different but not that it would necessarily lead to a different meaning. It is said that birds will nest with equal contentment on trees planted as a grid or in irregular clumps, and I suspect that the garden's situation within a Zen temple—with its attendant role to support meditation—overrides the actual configuration of the stones, at least in terms of meaning. On the other hand, Herrington is correct in suggesting that the stimulus to our readings would certainly differ. Given their alignment in a straight line we would probably not try to read the stones as "islands in an ocean" or "a bear and her cubs crossing a stream"—which have been offered as possible interpretations for the garden in the past. There would be new readings to be sure, like "a beam of light crossing the sea."[14] But are these readings coincident with differing meanings?

At this point we all seem to differ in our definitions of meaning although our implicit definitions overlap, at least to some degree. As described above, some authors suggest that body and mind are tied together, some separate cultural from individual meaning, others look at where signification lies. Obviously, and perhaps sadly, we have all been loathe to provide a concise definition of meaning and so even the very question itself will be open to multiple interpretations.

Rather than looking for parallels, similarities, or differences with the written word we might look instead, however briefly, at intention and meaning in the world of art. A recent issue of the Tate Gallery's house journal published a roundtable discussion with the four artists nominated for this year's Turner Prize and moderator Darian Leader.[15] While it is always somewhat unfair to extract quotations out of context, here are four that relate to the subject at hand.

> Lucy Skaer: *I always make my shows bearing in mind how the viewer will walk around them. I try to orchestrate that experience in a way that will make the work more open.*
>
> Roger Hiorns: *When I was working on the* Seizure *project last year, I had this desire to step back as far as possible from the actual viewer. I was concerned about 'contamination' from the viewer, from their relationship to something I'd made. That I had no interest in their experience of the work.*
>
> Enrico David: *I don't think too much about the audience, because if I do, I feel antagonistic towards them. I have no desire to entertain or be appreciated. I am searching for something which makes me feel assured within myself, regardless of or even in spite of the audience.*

Richard Wright: *I work from the principle that if the paintings have changed me, then it is possible that they would work on someone else. I begin by trying to convince myself that I am the audience, if you like. Maybe this supposes empathy, but the idea that I am trying to create meaning is not one that I really accept. It is more a question of participating in meaning.*[16]

These four quotations, which immediately followed one another in the artists' discussion, to some degree map out the difficult territory with which we are dealing and the response to the task by the maker —whether artist or landscape designer. Certainly we know that landscape architects bear environmental and social responsibilities with which artists need not be burdened. In that sense the artist is privileged to oppose society if he or she so desires—in a manner that client-sponsored projects will rarely permit. But the artists' conversation also illustrates the range of responses to the question of meaning and its production.

It is important here to distinguish between expression and communication. Expression emanates from the individual and may be a one-way street, that is, using forms appropriate to the artist while alien or even uncanny to the viewer. Communication, in contrast, implies a two-way street, requiring that both sender and receiver share a knowledge of the same code so that the message is received and decoded with as little distortion as possible. Should the audience be unfamiliar with the intentions of the painter they may interpret the work in wildly divergent ways—and from those interpretations derive their meanings. But it rarely will be the meaning intended by the maker. From this we may rightfully question whether the maker can invest any work—painting or landscape—with meaning, and if not, how does meaning result?

As Susan Herrington notes, perception is a key part of the process, and just the experience of a solid blue panel à la Yves Klein may come to mean something to the individual. Laurie Olin would question which part of meaning the viewer's perception governs: the "natural" meaning or the "synthetic" meaning: that is, just where is meaning vested? Jane Gillette suggests that the actuality of the blue panel and its effect upon our senses is more important than its maker's message, should there have been one. Yes, in time meaning may ensue but it is probably not the meaning intended by the maker, if—and that's a big if—the maker ever intended one. Perhaps the maker was just addressing pragmatic or hermetically aesthetic issues or perhaps even those of pure pleasure.

Given the long and broad history of philosophical debate on all matters of existence, the issue of meaning, too, will find no agreement, no single answer. Jane Gillette notes in her commentary that "despite small refinements, the issues addressed by theory are never solved. Far from proving anything, theory provides talking points for a conversation that is endlessly ongoing. Students need to be educated in these talking points because they will encounter the conversation for the rest of their lives."[17] In a collection of his essays, John Cage related an anecdote concerning Daisetz Suzuki, the great philosopher of Buddhist thought. After a stimulating discussion at a lively dinner party—with subjects of discussion that ranged from "a certain Indian yogi" to "the allegiance to Indian thought and to Japanese thought" to James Joyce and Gertrude Stein—the gathering concluded. "About eleven o'clock," Cage writes, "we were out on the street walking along, and an American lady said, 'How is it, Dr. Suzuki? We spend the evening asking you questions and nothing is decided.' Dr. Suzuki smiled and said, 'That's what I love about philosophy: no one wins.'"[18]

And one might add, no one loses either.

It should be noted that although tackling a philosophical subject—meaning—the authors are not philosophers and that both their method

xvii /

and conclusions may lack the rigor characteristic of investigations within the discipline of philosophy. These essays instead comprise the ideas of authors, educators, and practitioners within landscape architecture, and as such they provide thoughts on the subject of meaning that may be lacking in writings by those beyond the borders of the field.

Meaning in Landscape Architecture is a compendium of thoughts from four authors writing as individuals over a period of twenty years; all four essays were originally published in *Landscape Journal*, the scholarly publication of the Council of Educators in Landscape Architecture. The book stems from a panel I organized at the annual meeting of the association held in Tucson, Arizona, in January 2009. For the first time, all four authors met in one place to review and discuss their ideas. I requested that each author prepare a fifteen-minute talk by way of an introduction, looking back at what he or she was thinking then and how their ideas might have evolved since the time of publication. Obviously Laurie Olin and I had the most to reflect upon given the time that had elapsed since our thoughts first saw print. Because their essays were more recent Jane Gillette and Susan Herrington had less to rethink and revise and instead commented more on the quartet of essays as a group or on basic principles. The panel enjoyed a large attendance and a number of audience members requested a copy of the participants' texts. This book began as a response to those requests.

With the exception of errors that came to light, the original essays have been printed essentially as they first appeared; however, many of the images are new and in some cases, their number reduced. The commentaries that follow each essay reflect the presentations at the panel discussion although they have been reworked and expanded for publication.

It is obvious that four essays, each written independently, can only raise and discuss issues rather than answer them conclusively. In addition, the reader will note how the authors vary in their very definition of meaning and how and where it might apply to the conception, design, realization, perception, and interpretation of landscape architecture—and more specifically, gardens. Despite these limitations we hope that as a group *Meaning in Landscape Architecture & Gardens* will provoke further thinking about significance in general, and landscape design significance in particular, as well as about the human consequences of how we think about our designs and how we realize those ideas.

I thank the authors for the time spent revising their essays and writing their commentaries, *Landscape Journal* for allowing the republication of the essays, Karen Madsen for her final copyediting—and at Routledge, Alex Hollingsworth for bringing the project to the light of day.

Marc Treib
January 2010

Note:
The specific page numbers cited in the endnotes to all the essays and commentaries refer to those of the original publication in Landscape Journal *and not to the essays as reprinted in this book.*

NOTES

1 Charles Jencks and George Baird, editors, *Meaning in Architecture*, New York: George Braziller, 1970.

2 Henry Glassie, *Folk Housing in Middle Virginia: A Structural Analysis of Historic Artifacts*, Knoxville: University of Tennessee Press, 1970.

3 Dylan Thomas, *A Child's Christmas in Wales*, New York: New Directions, 1954, unpaginated.

4 Ian McHarg, *Design with Nature*, Garden City, NY: Doubleday, 1969.

5 Susan Herrington notes that she first took courses in architectural theory at Harvard because courses in landscape architecture theory were not offered. Email, 31 December 2009.

6 Mark Francis and Randolph T. Hester, Jr., editors, *The Meaning of Gardens: Idea, Place, and Action*, Cambridge, MA: MIT Press, 1990.

7 Ann Whiston Spirn, Editorial, *Landscape Journal*, Number 2, 1988, p. ii.

8 Laurie Olin, "Form, Meaning, and Expression in Landscape Architecture," *Landscape Journal*, Number 2, 1988, p. 149.

9 Ibid., p. 151.

10 Ibid., p. 159.

11 Marc Treib, "Must Landscapes Mean? Approaches to Significance in Recent Landscape Architecture," *Landscape Journal*, Number 1, 1995.

12 Jane Gillette, "Can Gardens Mean?" *Landscape Journal*, Number 1, 2005.

13 Susan Herrington, "Gardens Can Mean," *Landscape Journal*, Number 2, 2007.

14 As it happens, Zen practice denies any direct interpretations, much less specific interpretations. That is not the purpose of the garden. See Marc Treib, "Attending," in Rebecca Krenke, editor, *Contemporary Landscapes of Contemplation*, London: Routledge, 2005, pp. 13–35.

15 Enrico David, Roger Hiorns, Lucy Skaer, and Richard Wright with Darian Leader, "Artists, Art, the Media, and the Public," *Tate Etc.*, Autumn 2009, pp. 92–107.

16 Ibid., p. 96.

17 Jane Gillette, "Commentary," p. 166.

18 John Cage, *Silence: Lectures and Writings*, Cambridge, MA: MIT Press, 1966, p. 40.

0-1

ENJOYING THE VIEW, BILTMORE HOUSE, ASHEVILLE, NORTH CAROLINA [MARC TREIB]

1.

Form, Meaning, and Expression in Landscape Architecture

Laurie Olin   [1988]

Historically, landscape design has derived a considerable amount of its social value and artistic strength from three aspects of the endeavor: the richness of the medium in sensual and phenomenological terms; the thematic content concerning the relationship of society and individuals to nature; and the fact that nature is the great metaphor underlying all art.

Human landscapes exhibit a complexity akin to living organisms. They are composed of disparate elements that form entities different from their parts; they inhabit real time and interact with their environment. They can be evolutionary, undergoing morphological change (e.g., trees growing and maturing with subsequent visual, spatial, and ecological changes), and can even die, both physically and metaphorically.

Recently, two important and, in my view, incorrect theoretical assumptions have become so ubiquitous

1-1

SWA GROUP, LANDSCAPE ARCHITECTS; ROBERT GLEN, SCULPTOR; WILLIAMS [MUSTANG] SQUARE, LAS COLINAS, TEXAS, 1984. [MARC TREIB]

that they have seriously weakened landscape architecture as an artistic field, despite its social utility. The first has been to confuse human landscapes and the needs and achievements they embody with natural landscapes and their processes. Students, teachers, and practitioners alike demonstrate a lack of understanding of the relationship between the author/artist/designer and the medium of expression; also, they fail to understand its limits, range, and potential on the one hand and display an ignorance of the formal issues within the field and an anticultural stance that eschews aesthetic concerns and their history on the other. The second assumption is a new deterministic and doctrinaire view of what is "natural" and "beautiful" that has replaced older, alternative, views that were equally doctrinaire. Couched in a born-again language of fundamentalist ecology, this chilling, close-minded stance of moral certitude is hostile to the vast body of work produced through history, castigating it as "formal" and as representing the dominance of humans over nature.

This failure to appreciate the formal possibilities of the field, typological repertoire, and potential content (allegorical, iconographic, symbolic, emblematic) that have been developed through history is encouraged in part by an anti-intellectual and anti-historical bias that runs deep in American society and the profession, and in part by the wide scattering of the built work in time and space. The difficulties that accompany the amount of travel necessary to visit this diffuse body of work are compounded by the difficulties of describing and recording the phenomenological nature of sites that possess even minimal complexity or subtlety. As long as I can remember, the vast majority of practitioners have espoused a functional and "problem solving" ethic that, although socially beneficial up to a point, has in effect asserted that mere instrumentality is sufficient in the creation of human environments, eschewing the more difficult issues that are raised if one also aspires to practice at the level of art.

In theory, the range of formal expression in landscape design could be as broad and varied in scope as that of the numerous landscapes, things, and events in the universe, if not more so, since one might presuppose an opportunity for new experiments and combinations of existing phenomena. The things we make might only be limited by the laws of physics, chemistry, and biology. As Buckminster Fuller once remarked, "The opposite of natural is impossible."[1] Yet despite the astonishing number of different landscape designs built since prehistory, there has emerged a finite, even limited, repertoire of favored formal strategies and expressions that have been applied to countless different and particular places through time.

EXPERIMENTATION IN CONTEMPORARY LANDSCAPE DESIGN

The principal reason for the limitation of formal expression thus far is predominantly cultural, although certain constraints in building materials and physical intervention transcend both art and technology. Water, when unrestrained, runs downhill; plants die when their biological needs are not met. Nevertheless, the choice of materials with which to build—soil, stone, cardboard, tin, etc.—is determined almost exclusively by social factors (economics, safety) and cultural factors (aesthetics). The stir created by revolutionaries in design is usually brought about by their transgression of what is culturally acceptable regarding the choice of material or form or composition.

Three recent American landscape designs that exemplify such transgression of convention, thereby attracting critical scrutiny, attack, and praise, are Martha Schwartz's Bagel Garden in Boston, SWA's (George Hargreaves) Harlequin Plaza in Denver, and SWA's (Jim Reeves and Dan Mock) Williams Square at Las Colinas near Dallas. These projects have followed other contemporary art and design fields in an attempt to broaden the range of acceptable (and serious) formal expression from that which is normative in the field. No one does this in the name of program, function, or biophysical imperative except as broadly defined—i.e., only if aesthetics and the risk taking that accompanies inquiry and a craving for change (to see what is around the next bend) are defined as functions. In fact, one of the things that all of these projects have in common is how little they use the most traditional materials and devices of landscape design, specifically plants and reference to natural landscapes. Their shock value derives from this abnegation of "normal" imagery and texture. They are "contrast gainers" that in every likelihood will lose their strength and energy over time as they become members of a new class of landscape designs that eschew dependence upon planting or direct reference to natural form for their organization. This is not to say that they do not refer to nature. They do, but indirectly, by reference first to other works of art that were more directly inspired by "nature." As in transmission of energy in other forms and media, there is at each step a loss and a dissipation of that energy.

One dilemma of much recent avant-garde landscape design is that, in the desire to reinvigorate the field, many have turned to devices or strategies that lead away from the central source of its power: Nature. In the attempt to avoid banality and transcend imitation, a crisis of abstraction has developed. By adopting strategies borrowed directly from other fields and by referring to work that is itself an abstraction from the referent, many contemporary landscape designers are producing work that is thin, at best a second- or third-hand emotional or artistic encounter.

MATERIALS

The work of Martha Schwartz (the Bagel Garden, and her mother's garden in Philadelphia), of Schwartz and Peter Walker (the Necco field installed temporarily at MIT), and Walker's Tanner Fountain at Harvard University raise the issue of palette [see figure 4-2].

They argue that landscape design can use a host of untried and unconventional materials. Garrett Eckbo and Gabriel Guevrekian pioneered this endeavor earlier in the twentieth century with mixed results. Both experimented with industrial materials as substitutes for traditional materials. One thinks of Eckbo's use of plastic panels (corrugated and otherwise) and various precast elements and shapes in lieu of wood arbors, masonry walls, and screens; his search for new colors, textures, and shadows; and his adoption of shapes from the School of Paris painters; or of Guevrekian, who substituted shiny metal spheres and crystalline polygons for shrubs in his remarkable *Garden of Light.*

Landscapes throughout history have predominantly been made of natural materials, with the objects and structures placed within them made from processed or manipulated natural materials. In the nineteenth century, iron, concrete, asphalt, and glass were added in the works of Lenné, Paxton, Alphand, Olmsted, and others. Recent projects of artist Robert Irwin—with ephemeral qualities that are both analogous and complementary to those of plants and the play of light and shade through their structure and surfaces, and the successful mingling of metal and wire with natural elements—should convince any thoughtful person that the problematic effort to expand and invigorate the palette with which we work is a worthy one. On the other hand, when one considers the overwhelming variety of plants and the almost endless variety of patterns that one can achieve with only a few colors and shapes of pavement stones, it is easy to understand why some of the most gifted designers in the field have spent their careers working with a limited palette that was self-imposed, gradually reducing their choices to fewer and fewer elements, thereby producing profoundly poetic works. In fairness, one must further remark that Schwartz and Walker have embarked upon a similar reductive regimen and that their exploration of tainted or unexpected materials and formal orders has been carried out with enormous self-control and restraint. The self-conscious, continual referencing to contemporary works of art rather than to the world itself, however, is a genuine weakness.

IMAGERY

Williams Square at Las Colinas, Texas, near the Dallas-Fort Worth airport, by Skidmore Owings and Merrill, SWA, and the sculptor Robert Glen, can be considered to have expanded the range of expression currently practiced by attempting to rescue rhetoric and imagery from the past, specifically that of baroque aquatic sculpture groups [figure 1-1]. This is a revisionist (even historicist) piece that makes the assertion that a landscape design composition today can include elements that are figurative and narrative, and that they can be heroic in scale and understandable to laymen of the region. This work of folk imagery—"wild horses"—is raised to a level of civic prominence with violent and illusionistic presentation. The frozen moment of the Hellenist tradition that was revived by Bernini and continued by the Vanvitelli in works such as Acteon and his dogs in the fountains at Caserta comes to mind. The little jets that forever record the splash of the hooves are a touch that both the dilettante and connoisseur of the eighteenth century would have liked.

COMPOSITION

At Harlequin Plaza, George Hargreaves and his colleagues used old and accepted materials and arranged geometric compositions that were new and startling to landscape design in America [figure 1-2]. The materials—stone, stucco, soil, plants, metal, and water —can all be found in the Bois de Boulogne and Central Park. What is new and different (and unsettling to

1-2

GEORGE HARGREAVES /
SWA GROUP,
HARLEQUIN PLAZA,
ENGLEWOOD, COLORADO,
1982.

[MARC TREIB]

many) is the compositional methods and devices employed. The composition is indebted to strategies developed in painting, especially surrealism. This is a landscape of displacement, distortion, and dislocation. There are echoes of Dalí and de Hooch, of de Chirico and Haight-Ashbury, of Latin America, and of the School of Paris. Things assume positions or weight that we don't normally expect. The floor, or pavement, which we usually expect to be a fairly neutral ground quietly holding everything in place, is not only a brightly contrasting and active surface, but its orthogonal patterns are skewed and begin to writhe under the comparatively weightless objects that break and interrupt it more than sit upon it. Walls rise and fall, or are pulled apart, the outsides of which are harsh. Inside, between two central walls, things are small, fragile, oddly domestic, and out of place. Regardless of one's personal pleasures and aesthetic preference, this is an effective and moving work. It stimulates and disturbs. It pleases and teases. It winks and talks tough. In this work we can see an old strategy that has led to a succession of design styles in painting and architecture. Style is largely concerned with the development of a set of formal characteristics that are common to a group of objects or works of art (Renaissance, Baroque, Rococo, Picturesque, Gardenesque, Deco, Modern, etc.). Once such a set of characteristics becomes obvious, at least to the point where a designer can consciously know how to achieve them, then it is only a matter of desire to be able to break from those conventions. Examples of how to break from the conventions of classical, beaux arts, and picturesque design composition lie all about us like beacons in the work of many twentieth-century artists, writers, architects, and musicians. Hargreaves simply stepped over that line and utilized several of the most common devices of our era —principally collage and distortion.

A CRITIQUE

I am a little uncomfortable with the results of all of these works, partly because of my own predilections regarding what I wish to make myself, but also because of my skepticism about either the position taken by the designer or the choice of subject or materials. Experimentation with new materials is desirable and Walker/Schwartz in their emulation of Frank Gehry and numerous sculptors such as Carl Andre are to be applauded. Walker's Tanner Fountain in front of the physics building at Harvard—which places a series of handsome glacial boulders within a field of asphalt and water, steam and an eerie hum—is a remarkable piece. In my opinion, it is stronger than many of Walker/Schwartz's other works because it refers more directly to the material that it abstracts: natural landscapes of violence and erosion. I would have arranged the stones differently—denser to looser and not so uniform and equal in space and stone sizes—and I would have set them within a sea of pebbles and smaller stones. This would, of course, have completely changed the effect and the meaning, which raises an important question: How can changing the spacing of the stones or the simple substitution of what is, after all, only the bottom of a basin (but it isn't really a basin either, which is important) change the meaning? Because we invest certain patterns and materials with particular ideas and meaning, especially regarding nature and man's works, these patterns are loaded with associations. In this case, the material—asphalt—and the uniformity of position between solid and void have an association in our culture with the mechanistic and artificial, even to the point of abhorrence; whereas stones and water are quintessentially "natural" and are almost universally enjoyed by people, both old and young. This juxtaposition of the abhorrent and the delightful creates a challenge to our expectations of what is normal or proper. Likewise, the mechanical repetition of the near grid and near randomness of the stones, which denies particularity of place and focus, is both ironic in its self-denial (it is a particular place and a focal point within its context) and alludes to the absolute infinity of matter and its extension throughout the universe—a clearly evocative and apt metaphor to find at the doorstep of an academic building devoted to the study of matter. This is a powerful and successful work, employing traditional artistic devices for the presentation of meaning, some of which are referred to above. There is more here, for those who take the time to consider, about the seasons, the mutability of matter—water, steam, and ice, for instance—the deception of appearances, the energy that comes unbidden from the earth or from the sky, volcanoes and seacoasts, and so on. The piece also raises questions about alternatives to conventional fountains with their cascades, basins and pools, copings, walls, and ornament. Although this design eschews planting, it relies for its success upon the circumstantial planting that exists there as its context. The trees and grass of its campus setting form a background, a benign cultural interpretation of "Mother Earth" against which this disruptive and stimulating composition is positioned. Like many so-called site sculptors such as Michael Heizer, Nancy Holt, Mary Miss, or Alice Aycock, who are enormously dependent upon the pre-existence of a broad, cohesive, often beautiful, natural or cultural setting in which to make their disruptive gestures or to build their mysterious large-scale objects, this fountain (and the early work of Martha Schwartz as well) are gestures that play off and against an environment but are not about—nor capable of—creating an environment beyond that of an extended object.

Denver's Harlequin Plaza confronts different expectations and raises other questions. How are we to regard a landscape of disorientation and alienation? Is surrealism an acceptable strategy to employ in constructing an ordinary part of the workaday world? Why or why not? Such thoughts first occurred to me upon seeing several projects of Aldo Rossi. These were visually powerful schemes (for housing and education) that were obviously sophisticated works of art. The most apparent source of Rossi's visual schemata is the early work of the Italian painter Giorgio de Chirico, whose haunting work I greatly admire. I balk, however, at its use for the design of everyday environments for family and civic life. I do so because the principal focus of these paintings is upon alienation and a hallucinatory and obsessive preoccupation with loneliness, self, and unfulfilled yearning. De Chirico's paintings are among the most poetic works created in the twentieth century, but it is debatable whether such private (even if universal) attitudes regarding alienation can and should be used as a basis for design of environments for dwelling. The other undiscussed aspect of Rossi's work is its familiarity with and nostalgic evocation of the architecture of twentieth-century totalitarianism, especially that of Fascist Italy and Germany. Do I think that Harlequin Plaza is crypto-fascist or perverse? No, but I do think it transgresses the boundary between what is acceptable and understandable in private and what is welcome and desirable in public. This does not imply a double standard but rather that we have different needs as individuals and as a group. What people may indulge themselves with on private estates may be of arguable justification when proposed for the public realm. My reaction has more to do with the rhetoric of coercion and gratuitous violence than it does with dreamlike distortions of traditional architectural elements. Harlequin Plaza is, nevertheless, a watershed in American landscape composition and imagery. It has opened up possibilities that did not seem to exist before its brash appearance.

The horses of Las Colinas, like the exuberant figure of *Portlandia* that hunkers (or floats?) above the entry to Michael Graves' celebrated bunker in Portland, Oregon—The City of Roses—attempt the retrieval of a distant trope from a society profoundly different from our own.

Several questions are raised by this revisionist work. Is any single image, regardless of its merits, adequate for civic contemplation and elevation to heroic scale in an era of so many powerful and multiple images? If the answer is yes, is this the one to be singled out for such an honorific situation? Or is it like so many by Andrew Wyeth, a work that is nostalgic in its emulation of the technique and appearance of authentic work of the past yet lacking in the authority of those works, an empty simulacrum of something else? Is it a daring and genuine piece bursting with disarming energy and innocence? Have its creators simply said that narrative and figurative sculpture used as the centerpiece of a public space is passé only until someone steps forward and dares to attempt it? Is this private plaza in this suburban office sprawl a public place? I am skeptical of this piece, which seems too pat, too sentimental, too much a product of Western cowboy commodity art of the sort that fills galleries throughout the Southwest with the kitsch that has devalued the work of Russell and Remington. The reason to devote attention to this design lies in its attempts to shift the boundary of what is acceptable, to retrieve an artistic strategy that has slipped beyond the grasp of the modernist norm. It is a powerful and evocative work; it has been embraced by the community and has been the recipient of an American Society of Landscape Architects award. It is art regardless of how lasting or great it may turn out to be. What authority it possesses comes from the cultural values and what form it has comes from art, not from nature or any fresh insight or abstraction therefrom.

LANDSCAPE FORM

Everything that exists has form. The words "formal" and "informal" as used in everyday speech are meaningless and an obstacle to a discussion about design, which by definition always contains formal properties of some sort. Where do forms come from? Forms come from forms first. Forms do not come from words. They cannot. Words can describe physical forms, but they do not (or did not) originate them; nor can they perform operations upon them. One must be familiar with a repertoire of forms before one can use them or manipulate them. This includes the forms found in nature and the forms of art, our art and that of others—other media, other cultures, other periods. In nature are all forms. In our imagination is their discernment and abstraction.

Art, and landscape architecture as a subfield of art, proceeds by using a known body of forms, a vocabulary of shapes, and by applying ideas concerning their use and manipulation. Landscape architecture, like other fields, evolves as it finds new ways to perform operations upon a particular corpus of forms—re-using, re-assembling, distorting, taking apart, transforming, and carrying forward an older set of forms—often quite limited in range, but constantly making new things with new meanings. Occasionally a few new forms will be let in or discovered, but more generally new material consists of the re-presentation or recombination of material that has been forgotten or has been deemed banal or out-of-bounds for some reason.

Once again, where does this repertoire of forms come from? As I have remarked elsewhere in a discussion about places and memory, the only thing that we can ever know for certain about the world is what exists now or has existed in the past. To make something new we must start with what is or has been and change it in some way to make it fresh in some way. To merely repeat or rebuild what has existed is not creative and does not advance the field, eventually devaluing what is repeated. How to make old things new—how to see something common and banal in a new and fresh way—is the central problem in art. Arthur Danto, in the essay "Works of Art as Mere Real Things," goes so far as to say that the central activity of art is to transform ordinary (or extraordinary) real things into things that are art, i.e., no longer ordinary or mere real things.[2] Examples range from representations of landscapes (say in Claude or Innes) to Marcel Duchamp's declaring a urinal or bottle rack to be artworks. The planting of trees in rows, whether good or bad, new or old, is an act of transformation and can under particular circumstances be art of a very high order.

Two of the greatest landscape designers that ever lived were André Le Nôtre and Lancelot Brown. Neither of these artistic giants invented the elements that comprise the parts of their greatest compositions. In the case of Brown, the meadows, clumps, and belts of trees, lakes, dams, classical pavilions, even the positioning strategies, all existed in the landscape gardens of his contemporaries and immediate predecessors [figure 1-3]. Nevertheless, he produced unique, startlingly fresh, and profoundly influential designs that still possess energy and authority. The elements he used can be found in the works of Kent, Bridgeman, and Wise and the villas of Rome, especially the *vigne* of the Villas Madama and Giulia, but it was his particular assemblage that blended these elements into cohesive and tightly structured (albeit large scale) compositions that were not episodic or disjointed, but plastic and "whole." The source of cultural authority for these pastoral compositions was literature (from classical verse to the Georgian poets) and graphic art (from Roman frescoes to Claude and the Dutch landscape school, especially Ruysdael, Hobbema, and Cuyp). Also, there was a predisposition on the part of his audience to understand and appreciate his constructions, both as sensual environs and as emblematic representations of agrarian social views.

For Le Nôtre, one could say the same thing. Every shape and form he used exists in seventeenth-century pattern books and in the sixteenth-century Italian and French gardens that he knew as a child and young adult. What then is so special and creative about his

1-3

LANCELOT BROWN,
PETWORTH PARK,
ENGLAND, 1751–1764.
[MARC TREIB]

work? Like Andrea Palladio in his work at Il Redentore or the Villa Rotunda, he is working in a tradition, using standard elements, yet the results are more than a skillful or interesting repetition, more than traditional. He was highly original. His invention is one of recombination and transformation, frequently accomplished through a jump in scale with the simplest of elements and unexpected juxtapositions. Take Chantilly as an example: every shape—oval, square, circle, rectangle, ramp, parterre, and cascade—can be found in any of a dozen Roman gardens of the sixteenth and seventeenth centuries [figure 1-4]. Part of the transformation was to take elements originally conceived as furnishings for terraces or small garden rooms adjacent to houses (admittedly villas and *palazzi*) and to change their scale, enlarging and frequently stretching them, and then to use these new figures to organize and unify entire estates or large tracts of land, reversing the relationship until the building was essentially a furnishing or embellishment of the landscape composition. This is true even when, as was usually the case, the building was the seed around which the enormous garden had grown. If Vaux-le-Vicomte and Versailles are two of his central and most fundamental creations, Sceaux and Chantilly are possibly his most original. This is largely because of the amount of transformation from prototype and the relegation of the chateau in each case to a peripheral or tangential relationship to the composition, especially in its relationship to the most important water elements that exist as if for themselves with the parks subservient and organized about them. Here the shape, spirit, and meaning of these axial bodies of water and verdure are transformed from those that preceded them in France and Italy, in his own work as well as that of others. The source of their energy and authority is similar to that of

1-4
ANDRÉ LE NÔTRE,
CHÂTEAU DE CHANTILLY,
FRANCE,
c. 1680+.
[MARC TREIB]

Brown's work: foreign precedent and aesthetic paternity (especially Roman literature, archaeology, and Renaissance masterworks) plus contemporary science, particularly optics. How does one go about doing such things? How did he know to do this? It is hard to say. It is obvious that he had to abstract, perhaps I should even say extract, the forms, the types of basin, terrace, and bosque from the works he was exposed to, from his practical and immediate experience, and from representations in views, prints, and plans. Then, too, there was probably a certain felicitous amount of chance and direction given by the society, his clients, their budgets, programs, and desires, as well as the capabilities and constraints imposed by the site, the climate, and technology.

If one returns to my opening thesis that the strength of landscape architecture derives from the fulsome sensual properties of the medium, its expression of the relationship of society to nature, and the centrality of nature as the *ur*-metaphor of art, it is not difficult to understand why the works of Brown and Le Nôtre are among the very greatest in the field. Despite their differences in geometric form and organization, both men worked with the same limited palette that reduced the elements of their designs to the most basic—earth, trees, turf, stone, water—and arranged them at a scale that dwarfed the individual and created an ambience that, if not resembling any natural scene, by its very extent, diversity, and texture possessed the attributes of one. It is difficult to exaggerate the impact of their work on one's sensibilities when on the spot, moving through their compositions. Artificial as they may be, ecologically simplified as they are, the effect is that of being in a landscape larger than oneself and beyond the immediate comprehension or control of oneself, of many of the feelings one has in a "natural" landscape—of light and space, of amplitude and generosity. Two generations apart, both men produced work that responded to a particular moment in the economy and social structure of their society, that could not be sustained beyond their own life and career, and that was impossible to imitate or extend. Both refer to agriculture—whether that of pastoral herds or forest plantations, irrigation, and drainage schemes—the larger organization of the cosmos and whether it is knowable or not. Both were masters of the simple detail and the subtle, complex, large design, thereby rendering their work truly analogous to the natural landscape. Redundancy and profligacy does not appear to have been a concern or issue, another natural analog. Neither ever designed or built a composition that visually or formally imitated nature; both abstracted their forms from nature, farming, and art. The lakes at Blenheim and Stowe, at Vaux-le-Vicomte and Versailles—all were, in part, responses to an abundance of rainfall, surface water, and poorly drained soils. Each one expanded or drowned the work of a predecessor with an uncanny sense of organic logic. Until one has actually seen these works, on foot with one's own eyes, one cannot appreciate their character, achievement, or worth. Students who know these works only from slides or plans in books have no idea what they are like. In this way they also resemble natural environments of great scale, beauty, and cohesion.

All of this may be true enough and still one might ask, where did the prototypes Le Nôtre found in the sixteenth-century Italian gardens come from? In large measure they derived from the villa gardens of ancient Rome, especially as codified in the great landscape villas of the first century C.E. These in turn seem to have been derived from earlier Eastern Mediterranean prototypes brought by Syrian and Greek architects working in the new Western centers of power and industry. If one examines these remote works and their formal repertoire, one finds a host of venerable and familiar geometric and organic shapes. Nearly every Bronze Age culture shows a predilection for compositions composed of prime geometric shapes, often elaborated into surfaces of intricate textures of lines, whorls, and abstractions of powerful ambiguity—circles, squares, triangles, and their elaboration, recombination, and distortion. Knowledge, power, and the religious beliefs of these peoples were often embodied in such images and diagrams. The evolution of social authority and power was coincidental with the development of theories of reality and technology. The elementary shapes found in nature and abstracted by humans were, for many centuries, both sacred symbols and the building blocks of secular analytical methods. Today, spheres and cubes, triangles and cones are not as charged with meaning as they once were. Nevertheless, their ancient lineage and indisputable primacy in the vocabulary of formal structures are still sources of considerable authority. In a world consisting of small towns, irregular construction, straw roofs, and few paved streets, surrounded by farms and wilderness, overlooking broad plains, vast oceans, and dwarfed by mountains, the perfection of a sphere or cube, and the order of geometric symmetries, were powerful inventions of the human imagination. Today, as an urban culture, housed continuously in a world of crisp Euclidian geometries and surrounded by a surfeit of machined surfaces extending in Descartean order to the limits of the horizon, it is the biomorphic shapes of nature—the blurry, unclear, compound, and complex forms of natural processes—that intrigue us with their mystery, promise, and atavistic energy. Perfection, regularity, and ancient geometries, especially those of classical Greece and Rome, have been drained of their energy owing to overuse and exposure. Despite recent developments in post-modern architectural endeavors they remain empty to us of their original meanings. Once great abstractions of nature itself, today they only refer to former leaps of imagination. They have become too far removed from their original source and inspiration to be anything but derivative and banal to us. An echo of their former power still occurs, however, when small children take these platonic solids in their hands and stacking them one atop another construct their first imaginary worlds, miniature structures that invoke and reflect aspects of their known and imagined world.

Even the most casual examination of forms used in Roman garden design and ornament reveals a direct and rich tradition of natural forms and abstractions from nature as well as representational images that assume the stature of figures. By figure I intend the meaning as defined by Alan Colquhoun who has differentiated the words form and figure approximately thus: form applies to "a configuration with natural meaning or none at all," where natural meaning signifies meaning without the overlay of an intervening interpretive scheme of a culture; figure applies to a "configuration whose meaning is given by culture."[3] This distinction implies that the synthetic invention of a figure organizes ideas and thus is both expressive and didactic. There are therefore two traditions, the formal and the figurative, which are almost never totally separated, indeed often inextricable. Each one, from time to time, seems to have more or less importance or dominance in a work and its intentions and success. Much of twentieth-century art could be said to have been interested to varying degrees with abstract formalism and its possibilities (or limits). Recently, considerable interest in a renascent figural exploration has been evident in all of the arts, including architecture and landscape design. The three examples of so called "post-modern" landscape experimentation with which I began are part of this renewed interest in the "figural" aspect of the landscape medium.

LANDSCAPES AND MEANING

The subject of meaning in human expressions of all sorts is a daunting one with an enormous literature. It is the province of numerous philosophers of widely opposed views (Husserl and Wittgenstein, for instance, or Kant and Hegel, Plato and Popper). Husserl seems useful as a starting point in this matter. In his first logical investigation he says, "each expression not merely says something, but says it of something; it not only has a meaning, but refers to certain objects. But the object never coincides with the meaning."[4] Immediately we are confronted with a thicket of words, definitions, and problems. Suffice it to say, we are interested in non-verbal expressions, those of landscape design and what they can mean. As Nelson Goodman put it in his stimulating discussion of style in *Ways of Worldmaking*: "Architecture, non-objective painting and music have no subject. Their style cannot be a matter of how they say something, for they do not literally say anything; they do other things, they mean in other ways."[5]

Despite the frequent use of the analogy of language and linguistic structures and operations (my own use of the concept "vocabulary of forms" above, for example), landscapes are not verbal constructions. They can express certain things, can possess symbols and refer to ideas, events, and objects extrinsic to their own elements and locus, and in certain circumstances can be didactic and/or highly poetic. How they do this is not well understood. That they do is. Recent issues of various art history journals or the publications of papers delivered at Dumbarton Oaks symposia are rich with examples of sympathetic and recondite readings of the meanings, iconography, and imagery contained in various landscapes, from classical antiquity to the modern era, both in the West and East. Particularly well-known examples are those of sixteenth-century Italy and Japan (Villa Lante, Villa d'Este, Ryoan-ji, Katsura, etc.).[6]

The fundamental questions concerning meaning in landscape design are probably the following:

What sort of meanings can landscapes convey or hold?

How do they convey or embody these meanings?

What, if any, correlation or relationship is there between the intention of the designer of a landscape regarding devices intended for meaning and the subsequent interpretation, reception, and understanding of this or other meanings by a viewer, user, or recipient of the landscape?

Concerning the first two of these questions, there seem to be two kinds of meaning or large categories that landscapes possess (in Alan Colquhoun's terms all of these are figural to a greater or lesser degree). The first kind is a "natural" or "evolutionary" meaning given to a landscape in the past or recent times. (I regret using the word "natural" but have no better term at hand as I hope will become clear.) Generally, these relate to aspects of the landscape as a setting for society and have been developed as a reflection or expression of hopes and fears for survival and social perpetuation. These often relate to particular places or features that are (or have been) sources of sustenance and danger, safety, and play, of stimulus and rest. The second category are those that I shall refer to as synthetic or "invented" meanings. These encompass most of the works of landscape design and represent our art. Often, however, these works refer to aspects or examples of the former non-designed, although culturally freighted, group of landscapes and their meanings. I don't mean to imply in this distinction that I think that those in the first category are not products of human activity and imagination. It is, after all, people who project ideas upon nature, who create values, systems, and structures of thought, not the other way around. Whatever meaning occurs in any landscape, natural or otherwise, is only that which has been created by society. This we have seen when cultures are in conflict, so tragically demonstrated when European invaders desecrated the sacred lands of the Native American people. In the mining of metals in the Black Hills of South Dakota one can see how invisible these powerful and elaborate meanings can be to those not of that society and its beliefs.

Archetypal settings developed in one culture and place after another have contributed to the repertoire of forms and meanings used as foundations or structural elements of subsequent synthetic, designed landscapes. These include landscapes of work, mysticism and worship, dwelling (both individually and as group settings), authority, pleasure, and death. Work settings have included pastoral and arable farms as well as piazzas, streets, and roads. Patterns and structures of simplicity and elaboration associated with agriculture have a powerful resonance in this category. Religious and mystical settings are frequently centered around unusual and dramatic landforms, large or prominent features that dominate regions, or sources of water and secret or inaccessible sites. Group settings related to dwelling and community have often included the piazza or forum type of enclave, clearings, commons, and partially bounded spaces. These become transformed into places invested with authority when combined with approaches, avenues, frontality for presentation, and distortions in scale. Places most associated with pleasure have been those that approximate or have inspired gardens or areas of floral and natural beauty and delight—grottos, pools, cascades and streams, bizarre and stimulating formation of rocks, landforms, plants, and water. Consistently these landscapes have induced feelings of fascination, awe, fear, contemplation, amusement, and delight—in short, visual and sensory interest and stimulations of all sorts.

Among the oldest and incontestably most meaningful landscapes are those that I would term "sacred" landscapes, those associated with spiritual values and especially those of the origin myths of ancient peoples: Ise and Itsukushima in Japan; Delos and Delphi, or Mt. Ida and Olympus in Greece; Clitumnus, Cumae, and Avernus in Italy; Yosemite and Shasta in California; etc. [figure 1-5].

Other sites have become special because of events that transpired there or persons who were associated with them. Battlefields and the scenes of natural or

1-5

TORII,
ITSUKUSHIMA, JAPAN,
12th C. (REBUILT).
[MARC TREIB]

human disasters are one example. These range from the ruins of ancient imperial pleasure grounds (Hadrian's Villa, Tivoli) through bucolic farms turned battlefield (Gettysburg, Pennsylvania), to sites not remarkable in themselves such as Walden Pond, which come to be shrines for those who have embraced a set of ideas associated with the place. In this last case ideas associated with freedom of the individual, contact with nature and its processes, self-reliance and traditions of civil disobedience and transcendental literature in America and England are all conjured up to the initiated by this scruffy glacial pond and its setting. Nothing of the sort is possible, though, for those unfamiliar with the writings of Thoreau.

In many cases the meaning assigned to these sites was not originally intended or anticipated. In others, particularly those dedicated to gods or believed to be the ancestral home of a people, it has been imposed or in some way intended toward the site, invested and cultivated through human action and designation. A recent example of such intentions with success (of sorts) has been the creation of the National Park System of the United States. Consider Yosemite, Niagara Falls, Yellowstone, the Grand Canyon, and the great peaks of the West, which were originally the sacred sites of Native American Indians and have become so to us—who, in the hundreds of thousands, annually make our pilgrimages to them. Other countries that have followed our lead do so with recreation and ecological values in mind, but probably not with the quasi-religious motives of those involved in the creation of our parks, especially the great Western preserves that initiated the system. John Muir, Frederick Law Olmsted, and others involved in the parks' creation shared a transcendentalist point of view and an urge to establish natural sanctuaries (sanctuary in the full sense of its meaning) for the consideration and reverence of nature and the American landscape in its most original, wild, and dramatic state. This was in part a reaction to the rapid urbanization and industrialization of the country and partly an urge to forge a creation myth for the rebirth of the nation after the horror of the recent civil war that had very nearly destroyed the nation. The strength and beauty perceived in these landscapes, their scale and character, was seen to be uniquely American and un-European; their association with native peoples as sacred or treasured sites also contributed to their being chosen. They were a balm and a stimulus. They were pure and innocent of human order. Protecting them from exploitation became a cause for intellectuals, liberals, and upper-class members of the ruling establishment. Yellowstone came first; other sites were added later: Niagara Falls, the Grand Canyon, Glacier, etc. This history is well known but rarely considered. These landscapes still have a number of meanings that can be read and articulated by some (but not all) members of our society and represent what I have referred to awkwardly as "natural" or "evolutionary" meaning in landscapes, whether of human construction or not.

Now let us turn to those landscapes that are constructed and for which we might consider meaning to be invested or synthetic as a part or product of our art. The methods of injecting meaning into a designed landscape range from creating tableaux with recognizable creatures and figures to abstract references implied by the structure or arrangement of non-representational elements totally unrelated to those to which the design refers. The content, or "meaning," of many of the most famous landscape designs often was established through the use of works of sculpture and architecture that already carried associations with or recognizable references to particular ideas and other works of art, literature, landscape, or society. The iconographic programs of the Villa Lante and the Villa Aldobrandini—with their classical figures and fountains expressing neo-Platonic concepts and suggesting or recalling passages from Ovid's *Metamorphoses* and classical mythology while referring to the patron, his family, and works

—are familiar to today's student of landscape history. The study of iconography in Renaissance art and architecture established by Panofsky and Wittkower has introduced the theory that a work can contain at least three levels of content:

1. The subject of the work—that which is present or constructed (denoted): it is a park, a garden, or a piazza, just as a painting presents a subject, say a bowl of apples or a Roman soldier with arrows sticking into him.

2. The reference of the work to things not present but invoked (connoted): a range of mountains that one cares for, the martyrdom of a saint, a time or moment that has passed, etc. The things that are connoted can be numerous, all at once; there can be multiple layers of reference within any particular image or composition, and often times the higher the art, the more such connotations there are.

3. A mood or feeling about these two previous things that is developed through expression or style. A garden, like a painting, can be somber or gay, witty or matter-of-fact. This is an issue that produces considerable confusion and hostility, for this aspect of design is the one that has the most to do with matters of change in taste and fashion, although the previous one is more closely related to the recent changes that attempt to reinvigorate the boundaries of the field of landscape architecture.

Goodman and Danto disagree in some respects concerning the effectiveness of meaning that can be intended. Some of the meanings that landscape designers of the classical tradition have carried include thoughts about duty and love for family and country (Stowe, Stourhead, Rousham) or have combined attitudes toward classical learning and the duties of the Christian church (Villas Lante and d'Este) or have explored themes of passion and love, of mental disorder and analogous forces in nature (Villas Farnesina and Bomarzo). Themes such as metamorphosis and transfiguration recur frequently, as do those of a hero overcoming a variety of obstacles, whether historic in neo-Platonic Christian overlays upon pagan tales as in the choice between virtues of Hercules in the Pantheon at Stourhead, or contemporary themes such as the rocky Calvinist path to the Temple of Wisdom and Piety (Apollo), also at Stourhead. The tradition of depicting and pointing out through the use of recognizable and symbolic elements, combined with the emotive and connotative device of naming things or places to insure the desired association or "reading" of landscape compositions, continued from the Renaissance until near the end of the nineteenth century. Consider an example: At the end of a long and stately mall of elms in Central Park—the principal geometric figure within the entire park—at a place where the most important pedestrian promenade intersects the principal carriage drive, at an overlook to a carefully contrived lake with a "natural" backdrop of a skillfully re-forested hillside (now known as The Ramble), the designers placed a remarkable fountain, piazza, stairway, and boat landing. The entire ensemble is presided over by a graceful angel, created in Rome by Emma Stebbins. The name given to this place is Bethesda Fountain [figure 1-6].

To the public today the name is not particularly emotive, but to the Christian, Bible-reading population of the years after the Civil War, the reference was a particularly meaningful one. Bethesda was the name of a basin in ancient Jerusalem that had five entryways. Its waters were considered to possess healing powers, and many who were ill, crippled, or in physical or mental distress came to bathe in it. The Apostle John related that one of Christ's miracles took place on this spot on a Sabbath, when a man too crippled to enter the basin on his own languished beside it (John 5:2). Christ told him to pick up his quilt and walk, whereupon he was able to do so. The result, of course, was to get Jesus in further trouble with the authorities for attending the sick on a holy day and for giving vent to the people's excitability, stirring up their expectations by this action. The representation of a source of cleansing, healing, and recovery was both personally (to Olmsted) and publicly an emotional and welcome message to be understood and appreciated by the citizenry regardless of class—not necessarily regardless of faith, of course. Additionally, parks were seen by Olmsted as performing a cleansing or purifying role within cities, an association of great lineage. Alberti and the ancients all have asserted the relative importance of nature as a therapeutic device. The central symbol of Central Park, therefore, is one of healing and purification.

This sort of representational and symbolic narrative was not to continue much longer in landscape design—at least in the most advanced design—in fact, not even in Olmsted's own work. Just as in the work of Capability Brown, there was a rapid evolution toward a more pure formal abstraction utilizing landscape structures to connote landscape imagery. This can be observed as early as Prospect Park and becomes more noticeable after Olmsted's separation from Calvert Vaux and the team of designers and craftsmen associated with the New York practice who exemplify many of the aesthetic propositions of Ruskin and Pugin. I refer to the more transcendental and abstract tendencies of Olmsted that are revealed in his proposals for Mount Royal in Montreal, Quebec; the Fenway and Muddy River designs for Boston; and the quasi-Southern marsh landscape he proposed for the south lake shore of Chicago, which became such an inspiration for Jens Jensen.

Let us consider some of the imagery of Prospect Park and its formal structure. Although much has been added and destroyed in this park to blur the original meaning and intent, I believe it can still be read and understood. Unlike Central Park, Prospect Park is not a patchwork quilt of objects and enter-

1-6

FREDERICK LAW OLMSTED, SR., BETHESDA TERRACE, CENTRAL PARK, NEW YORK CITY, c. 1854; EMMA STEBBINS, SCULPTOR; BETHESDA FOUNTAIN, 1873. [MARC TREIB]

tainments stitched together in a rectangular setting or frame—episodic and jumbled. Instead, it has a purposeful and plastic structure derived from the landform (Calvert Vaux was the genius here), which has been developed with only a few major features and themes, each of which was then furnished to the degree appropriate to its use and purpose, with a careful eye to mood and thematic unity. The principal parts are the Long Meadow and woodland belts that define it; the broad lake and its shore; and a tumbled rocky set of ravines, ledges, and highlands that both separate and connect these first two. Within this wilder and more "natural" portion stands an enormous, crude, and puzzling structure. It is a bridge carrying a pedestrian trail over a stream and bridal path, unlike anything produced by the Olmsted consortium up until then. Its rude form should not be mistaken for accident, poverty, or lack of sophistication, for nearby stands the music terrace, a feature analogous to Bethesda Terrace, replete with elaborately conceived and carved walls, piers, and sculpture with ornament derived from native American flora and geology similar to that at the U.S. Capitol in Washington, D.C., and in Central Park. This sophisticated site with its busts of composers such as Beethoven, faces west, out across the water of the lake, to receive the full reflection of the late afternoon and setting sun.

Returning to the comparatively Paleolithic structure of Boulder Bridge, we are faced with a problem of meaning and intention. What are we to make of it? Crude things go with wild places? In a way, yes, but much more than that. Earlier in Central Park, the same office had produced one elegant and delicate bridge after another with details of resplendent and enthusiastic character, bursting with life and references to nature and its processes, especially vegetation, with floral motifs, rosettes, entwined branches, and so on.

The relationship to Morris and Ruskin, to the roots of art nouveau, is everywhere evident. But in this park all of the bridges are different in mood or expression from those of Central Park, as are all of the landforms. Larger, simpler, more robust, several of the bridges are made of heavy industrial members, evocative of railways, ships, boilers, and the new heroic machines of the day. They are, however, touched with a few grace notes of a particular sort of ornament— the sort one associates with Frank Furness and Louis Sullivan— of singular floral motifs, often only in one place and low down near the pressure point, the contact area between the engineered object and the earth. The machine devoted to human and social purpose is portrayed as an outgrowth of man and as a creature of nature. Earlier there had been a few hints, as in the partial step cut into a rock ledge in The Ramble, of an attitude of man in nature as co-worker, making minimal gestures, and of nature completing the art. Later Olmsted wrote in his Montreal report:

> When an artist puts a stick in the ground, and nature in time makes it a tree, art and nature are not seen apart in the result… the highest art consists, under such circumstances, [in] making the least practicable disturbance of nature; the highest refinement in a refined abstinence of effort; in the least work, the most simple and the least fussy and pottering.[7]

In my view, Prospect Park is a meditation on post-Civil War America. It presents Olmsted's renewed inspiration drawn from the scenery of the Far West as well as his emotional transcendentalism: on the one hand, the grandeur and roughness of the landscape and yearnings for peace and prosperity, and on the other hand, his desire for agriculture and industry that serve the needs of the nation while producing graceful, livable cities.

Boulder Bridge does not stand for any one thing. It is a contributing element to a larger fabric, a mysteriously geological and non-cultural detail, ambiguous and heavy, the metamorphosis of boulders into the semblance of a bridge. In this fashion his later work can be seen as poetic and emblematic in much the same way as those of Brown and Repton. Unlike Kent and Hoare, or other earlier connoisseur-designers whose work presented its meaning through a series of tableaux of silent assemblages of pavilions, inscriptions, evocative sculpture, and titles, Olmsted moved to a more abstract and sophisticated presentation. This is partly because the ideas to be presented made reference to other landscapes and to their meaning for society, not to stories about gods or patrons, and had more to do with general concepts of the medium, the expression of physical properties, and the manipulation of them as part of the presentation (the denotation) and as an embodiment in these works of the formal ideas that were contained within the earlier and more anecdotal narrative landscapes. In this development, he had retraced the evolution of the strategy of presentation and analogous content of the Japanese stroll gardens (which he never saw).

RHETORIC AND METAPHOR IN LANDSCAPE DESIGN

Regarding expression, one must address "rhetoric" and "metaphor" in landscape design. If works of design can be considered to refer to things that are not present and can do so while establishing a particular mood or feeling, then those devices that are used to suggest, persuade, or lead an audience to the desired conclusion are what has been called rhetoric. A rhetorical question is used to make a statement not by stating it, but rather by leading the listener to complete the thought, to reach what might at the time or situation created by the author of the rhetorical question appear to be the obvious or "natural" conclusion. Aristotle, who understood such things as well as anyone ever will, believed that rhetoric consisted of those effects that seek to arouse certain attitudes toward whatever is being presented (he was mostly referring to verbal structures). In his view rhetoricians must have a sufficient understanding of human sensibility and emotion so that they can sufficiently characterize an action or an object to induce the desired response in their audience, i.e., anger, sympathy, distress, patriotism, etc. "It is not enough for a rhetorician to demonstrate that a certain feeling ought to be felt, or that his audience would be justified to feel it and perhaps unjustified not to feel it: he is only worth his salt if he gets them to have that emotion and does not just tell you what you should be feeling."[8] The devices and strategies that designers use to manipulate a setting and its furnishings in order to produce responses are many and normally involve a remarkable amount of craft and learning. As in every other art a certain amount of feeling and instinct for the medium and its devices are necessary. To this, one must then add a level of performance ability before one can begin to manipulate or discuss style, expression, and meaning. Consider the phenomenon of rhetoric in the art of building design. Many critics, historians, and philosophers have commented upon the "verticality" of Gothic cathedrals and the fact that this expression of the idea of verticality, this property that has been invested in the inert materials through the manipulation of form, structure, and detail, gives these buildings a property that is not possessed by other buildings. Furthermore, in some ways this "vertical" characteristic that we read in these buildings is linked to metaphors for soaring, rising up from and leaving the earth in some manner similar to ideas held by the people of the religion that built them and that were associated with the progress of the human soul after death as well as the assumption of the resurrected Christ and his mother into Heaven, which was poetically considered to be away from the earth, up above the clouds in the sky or heavens.

The piety and yearning for release from life on earth was embodied in these structures through numerous strategies of design related to the suppression of architectural motifs that normally connote mass or weight and which emphasized verticality over horizontality through distortion, stretched proportions, segmentation of structural masses into what appear to be bundles of tall thin elements, etc. That the arrangement of parts and their articulation and shape can change more than a building's appearance is an established theory of architectural practice and analysis of our time. Alan Colquhoun, Kenneth Frampton, Anthony Vidler, Robert Venturi, Peter Eisenman, and Jorge Silvetti have written eloquently and at considerable length about the rhetoric and devices of twentieth-century architecture and its predecessors. Very little has been written about the rhetorical devices employed in landscape architecture, especially by its greatest practitioners. Hamilton Hazlehurst and Kenneth Woodbridge are among the few who have tried. Even less has been written about such matters in contemporary practice. The entire effort is clouded by the nature of the medium. The fact that natural materials, some of them alive, are frequently used to represent aspects of nature and landscape (i.e., the referent and referee may be made of the same substance) greatly complicates matters. This is especially so when one turns to the most powerful rhetorical device: metaphor.

The most common and persuasive poetic device used in all fields of art is the metaphor; indeed, metaphor seems to be almost synonymous with art. Metaphor is commonly described as a figure of speech in which a name or descriptive term is transferred to some object to which it is not properly applicable. There must, therefore, be an untrue equation. It is the describing or presentation of one thing in terms of another. It is not literally true at all, but there is a discovered truth or insight that does in some way make sense and gives us a new understanding of the world or some aspect of it, whether small or large, funny or tragic. The old clichés that use a river as a metaphor for time or life are examples; Shakespeare's phrase "all the world's a stage" is another; or Kenneth Koch's student who in error penned the masterpiece, "a swan of bees." In *The Transfiguration of the Commonplace* Arthur C. Danto describes at great length the mechanisms of metaphor and its centrality to the creation, meaning, and understanding of all art. It would be foolish either to attempt a synopsis or to paraphrase this remarkable essay. I refer readers to it.[9] In his view one thing essential to the workings of metaphor is a phenomenon of incompleteness and correlation upon which the audience must react for the metaphor to work. In important ways this is related to and partially derived from the "rhetoric" employed by the artist/designer. It is also conditioned by the education, experience, and attitudes of the audience. Therefore, as education, experience, and beliefs change, metaphors can die, lose their potency, become clichés or stale figures of speech, design, or art.

It is also through the evolution of society and education, knowledge and values, especially as stimulated by historians, critics, and artists, that dead or lost metaphors can be revived. It seems, therefore, that there is a guaranteed tension between the nature of art (its processes of renewal, evolutionary transformation, and the potency of its metaphors) and the accessibility or immediacy of its meanings in a changing society. This process has intensified in recent decades. As Clement Greenberg has commented, "modernization" in art has largely consisted of discarding expendable conventions.[10] As long as conventions survive and can be identified, they will be attacked. This will continue until the resultant work begins to deny its own essence or can no longer be understood to be art in the form or medium as previously intended. In the view of many people, painting and music have come to a halt for now, in terms of formal invention and revision, and can only retrace various aspects, nooks, and crannies of their historical corpus—appearing to have reached the limits of their recognizability and validity. The same cannot yet be said for the architecture of landscapes and buildings.

Often the most "advanced" artists do not set out to be revolutionary or advanced, but rather to be good. The "advance" comes from an emulation of those qualities that they admire in previous work. As a rule, having digested the major art from the preceding period or periods, the young artist or designer usually looks for alternative ones in order to break away from overpowering precedents. In landscape design it would appear that a moment has arrived where many practitioners and students are looking for alternatives to conventions that are perceived to be empty and used up. Some (as I have remarked earlier) have turned to the conventions of art. This, however, is to place oneself in a secondary or derivative relationship to the fundamental source of form and imagery in the field, i.e., the world of nature, natural processes, and the cultural landscapes of the past, whether sacred, agricultural, or ornamental.

Several of America's most original and powerful landscape designers of the twentieth century appear to have drawn upon these primary sources. Richard Haag, A. E. Bye, and Lawrence Halprin have all produced direct fresh abstractions of natural phenomena. Thomas Church and Dan Kiley have done the same with particular landscapes and gardens of the past. All of these individuals have understood the need to abstract and distill formal essences without imitating or building miniature encapsulated versions of the source of their inspiration. Their work represents the first truly fresh development (both stylistically and formally) since the late eighteenth century.

A. E. Bye has produced some of the most abstract work, for instance the Soros garden in Southampton on Long Island, which looks neither like a painting, nor a garden, nor a natural landscape. It is truly a composition that could only exist in the landscape medium. It is pared down and yet deeply sensual. Its subject matter is the earth and its surface is delineated by light, the texture of plants, and water in all of its forms—mist, water, and snow.

Haag, too, has plumbed the depths of our urban and rural psyches, maneuvering the city of Seattle into leaving the monstrous heart of a gas refinery as a colossal memento mori in the center of a park on Lake Union. Despite a citizenry that wanted to build a pseudo-sylvan realm, Haag subverted the plan into an archaeological playground of genuine meaning and poetry. This park now exists and may come to be a fine one, in a conventional sense, in terms of its verdure and facilities. But it also has a sculpture many times more powerful than all the site artists in America could make, one that speaks to us about our past in ways that only the broken aqueducts and fallen columns of ruined temples can. There is no foolishness, no sentiment, no false note. There is also no other urban park quite like it.

Elsewhere, in the woods of Seattle's Bainbridge Island on the Prentice Bloedel estate, Haag quietly labored for over fifteen years on another highly personal and startlingly fresh series of landscape studies [figure 1-7]. Linked to each other and to the place, they constitute an extended essay on the making of landscape compositions. Most are produced by a strategy of subtracting from the second-growth forest. Several examine traditional devices of the Orient: moss gardens and miniature abstractions that dwarf the adjacent larger landscape, the stroll sequence of views; or Western conventions: the reflecting ponds, hedges, and geometries of the Renaissance, the invented naturalism of the eighteenth century (in this case a seemingly natural pond created to attract blackbirds for the pleasure to be had in their song), and so on. I know of no other person who could so cunningly create a garden room in the forest presided over by a haunting collection of moss-covered stumps that stand as gaunt reminders of the primeval forest that once stood there on what is now the estate of one of America's wealthiest timber barons [figure 1-8].

Haag's work, like that of an old Zen monk (which he at times resembles), confounds us with its apparent directness and subtleties.

Like Song dynasty scrolls or an old koan, it seems to grow directly from experience and the forces of nature. The artist has somehow stepped back out of the picture. It seems simple, yet contradictory. What had been a swimming pool and terrace have disappeared. In their place a great mound of white marble chips has appeared, next to a hole in the ground—also with white stone chips. This act of quiet displacement sits within a green sea of grass. The terrace itself has been sawed up into bits, some of which remain drifting about in this lawn. Like fragments of a shattered planet they move away from the center of the space and appear to orbit the haunting white pyramid. This in turn is encircled by planted mounds which, in their color and texture, appear like distant mountains. Beyond these, the light filters through clearings and deep vistas that Haag arranged far off into the woods of Agate Point. This composition demonstrates a mastery that grows out of a lifetime of developing abstract representations. Haag's Bloedel designs are among the most powerful works of this century in their exploration of the relation of gardens to nature. It is only to be lamented that the University of Washington has recently destroyed or mutilated several portions of his unfinished masterpiece.

Almost as the alter ego to this quiet work executed *in media rus* stands the exuberant and equally inspired work of Halprin, which burst forth in the heart of numerous American cities in the 1960s and 1970s, most notably in Portland and Seattle. Long after this one-man theater, workshop, circus, and human dynamo is gone, the work will remain, the best of which is superior to all of its imitations around the world. It is no surprise to those who know of the many years of residences (e. g., McIntyre in California) and suburban shopping centers (e.g., North Park, Dallas) that Halprin cranked out, that his work is genuinely intended for the pleasure and use of people. His celebrated fountains (several

1-7

RICHARD HAAG,
REFLECTION POOL,
BLOEDEL RESERVE,
BAINBRIDGE ISLAND,
WASHINGTON, 1979–1984.
[MARC TREIB]

of which derive a considerable amount of their character from the sensibility and intelligence of Angela Danadjieva who worked on them under his direction) are both an extension of the European baroque public fountain tradition and a departure from it, conditioned by their American context [figure 1-9]. Halprin himself has been quite articulate about the sources of form and imagery in this work: the high Sierras and their glaciated valleys, boulders, torrents, and meadows; the carved cliffs and headlands of the Pacific coast from California to the Northwest; the overwhelming human creations and devastation of granite quarries; and a couple of the great Italian fountains, especially the central passage of the water organ of the Villa d'Este at Tivoli. The Portland Auditorium Forecourt Fountain and the one built over a freeway in Seattle are not pastiches of this source material, however, but deeply organic and plastic creations. Echoes of the sources of their inspiration reverberate through the massing and even the shape and batter of the monoliths, plinths, and buttresses over and down which the water cascades. Nowhere does this work really imitate or literally represent or even look like its antecedents, either natural or cultural. Halprin—like Bye, Haag, and Kiley—adamantly rejects the possibility that one can or should imitate nature. One should be inspired by it, emulate its logic, generosity, processes, and forms, but eschew attempts or desires to copy it; all of them have said this in their words and affirmed it in their work.

The largest and most radical break from the past in our time has been our attitude toward composition—the conventions of order. Traditionally, in European art there has been a strong tendency to bring diverse elements of any work into a balanced composition, replete with harmony and symmetry (often in several dimensions), to complete a whole that reaches a degree of resolution and finality. This can be done with exuberance and

1-8

RICHARD HAAG,
MOSS GARDEN,
BLOEDEL RESERVE,
BAINBRIDGE ISLAND,
WASHINGTON, 1979–1984.
[MARC TREIB]

considerable movement and formal complexity as in the great baroque works, or with a calm, quiet, restraint of form and shape approaching near stasis as in certain neoclassical gardens and buildings. In a statement admired and quoted by F. L. Olmsted, the French landscape architect Édouard André notes: "The first law of a work of art, either on canvas or on the earth, is to be a whole."[11] Although that may still be true enough, the criteria of what is an acceptable whole are probably very different today than in his time. Twentieth-century art has opened new possibilities that have become part of our mental equipment, significantly altering our visual sensibilities. Cubism, for instance, introduced the now commonplace idea that multiple points of view can exist within a single work of visual art and that apparent conflicts between them do not need to be resolved. Collage has introduced further study of the relationship between representation and illusion and between that of the fragment or part to the whole while utilizing a combination of mass-produced images and handmade or pre-industrial craft gestures as raw materials for representation. The results have been the recombination of shattered or dislocated fragments into something other than that of their origin. This use of real rather than rendered material, when translated into the use of ready-made industrial items or the use of things that are meant to be absent yet referred to but are in fact present, has a direct bearing upon landscape architecture. This ironic position when taken toward the tradition of representation and the surplus of images in our society has only begun to filter into the field. Fletcher Steele, Gabriel Guevrekian, and Garrett Eckbo certainly have broken some ground here but only recently have Walker, Schwartz, Hargreaves, Van Valkenberg, Weintraub, and a new generation, especially on the West Coast, begun to mine this rich vein of ideas. Fragmentation, dislocation, displacement, and distortion

1-9

LAWRENCE HALPRIN, AUDITORIUM FORECOURT FOUNTAIN, PORTLAND, OREGON, 1967.

[MARC TREIB]

have all become acceptable strategies for design manipulation of traditional material and imagery, and they are central in efforts currently underway as the field renews itself. The schools are full of students experimenting with these strategies, and we will probably be awash in work, much of it not very good, that attempts to put it into practice. Nevertheless, it is probably for the best. Inevitably this will lead some back to a re-examination of the plant palette, landform, and natural process. The forms available to cast this material into compositions, however, may partake of the new structures revealed through the telescope and microscope ranging from those of recombinant DNA to the most archaic obstructions of the Bronze Age and tomorrow's computer technology.

The subject matter or meanings that I believe are being dealt with in the most thoughtful landscape designs today—beyond the programmatic and instrumental—are the following:

1. Ideas of order

2. Ideas of nature including a critique of past views as provoked by knowledge of ecology

3. Ideas about the arrangement of cities and thereby society and its desires (as well as needs)

4. Ideas about the medium as an expressive one (the landscape as medium) revealing something about our methods and its processes

5. Considerations about the history of art and landscape design and the history of places—their archaeology.

In these, the design expression is often a critique of past designs and landscapes. Many of the best works of the moment are inquiries into the validity of past expressions and their extension into the present, as well as being new and healthy creations of their own. One need only think of Richard Haag's Gasworks Park and Bloedel Reserve gardens in Seattle to realize the validity of this statement. In works like these one sees that the sensual properties of the medium are undiminished, that it continues to carry an expression of our ideas about nature and our place in the scheme of things. Finally we see the power of fresh abstractions and how futile are the attempts to replicate nature—in fragment or in toto—as a design method or a goal.

AUTHOR'S NOTE:

If this article hadn't become so long I would have liked to present some of the recent work of our firm to demonstrate particular aspects of how we have attempted to introduce some of this into our practice. Another article, particularly dealing with recent works, seems to be more appropriate.

NOTES

1 The author first heard Fuller say this in a public lecture at Columbia University in the spring of 1965. The concept pervades much of Fuller's work and writing.

2 Arthur Danto, *Transformation of the Commonplace*, Cambridge, MA: Harvard University Press, 1981, pp. 1–32.

3 Alan Colquhoun, "Form and Figure," *Oppositions 12*, Spring 1978, pp. 29–37.

4 Edmund Husserl, *Logical Investigations*, J. N. Findlay, translator, New York: Humanities Press, 1970, p. 267. See also J. N. Mohanty, "Husserl's Theory of Meaning," in Frederick Elliston and Peter McCormick, editors, *Husserl Expositions and Appraisals*, South Bend, IN: University of Notre Dame Press, 1977, p. 18.

5 Nelson Goodman, *Ways of Worldmaking*, Cambridge, MA: Hackett Publishing Company, 1978, p. 23.

6 See David Coffin, editor, *The Italian Garden*, Washington, D.C.: Dumbarton Oaks, 1972, especially Elisabeth MacDougall, "*Ars Hortulorum*: Sixteenth Century Garden Iconography and Literary Theory in Italy," pp. 37–59; or Coffin's own study of the Villa Lante: *The Villa in the Life of Renaissance Rome*, Princeton, NJ: Princeton University Press, pp. 347–351. There are numerous books that discuss Japanese gardens. One of the best remains Masao Hayakawa, *The Garden Art of Japan*, New York: Weatherhill and Tokyo: Heibonsha, 1973.

7 Frederick Law Olmsted, "Montreal: A Mountain Top Park and Some Thoughts on Art and Nature," in S. B. Sutton, *Civilizing American Cities*, Cambridge, MA: MIT Press, 1971, pp. 204–206.

8 Danto, *Transformation of the Commonplace*, p. 169.

9 Ibid., pp. 163–208.

10 Clement Greenberg, "American Type Painting," in *Art and Culture*, Boston: Beacon Press, 1961, pp. 208–229. This remarkable essay explores the notion that the American Abstract Expressionists managed to make explicit matters that were left implicit in previous European painting and vice versa.

11 Quoted in David Bellman, "Frederick Law Olmsted and a Plan for Mount Royal Park," *Mount Royal, Montreal, Supplement #1, Canadian Art Revue*, Ottawa, Canada, 1977, pp. 53–57. The catalog accompanied an exhibition of the same name at the Musée McCord, McGill University, Montreal.

1-10

PETER EISENMAN, ARCHITECT; LAURIE OLIN, LANDSCAPE ARCHITECT; MEMORIAL TO THE MURDERED JEWS OF EUROPE, BERLIN, GERMANY, 2005. [MARC TREIB]

Commentary 1:

What Did I Mean

Then or Now?

Laurie Olin

meaning *n. 1. That which is intended to be, or actually is, expressed, or indicated; signification; import; the three meanings of a word. 2. the end, purpose, or significance of something; What is the meaning of life? What is the meaning of this intrusion?...*[1]

Some time ago, in fact twenty years ago—almost longer than I can believe—I published "Form, Meaning, and Expression in Landscape Architecture" in *Landscape Journal*.[2] It was largely derived from lectures I'd been giving at Harvard's Graduate School of Design. It was heartfelt and I hoped at the time for it to be an overdue correction to what I perceived as a prevailing view in the field, namely that landscape architecture was or should be primarily a field of problem solving, largely based upon applied sociology and ecology. Against my better instinct my first partner had written into an early office brochure that we didn't believe in "art for art's sake" in landscape design.[3] At that time only a handful of practitioners not related to or involved in academia, or the training and education of landscape architects, believed or acted upon the premise that it was or could be examined as art.

The impact of land art and the anti-museum, anti-object, out-of-the-gallery and studio, out-of-bounds, sculpture movements of the 1970s were a shock and wake-up call. It announced to the profession that in terms of expression one could do much more with a piece of land than merely solve technical and functional problems. It was not a surprise, however, to those who knew much about the history of landscape and garden design. A general anti-intellectual attitude and ignorance of the history of architecture, art, and landscape — due to the preponderance of landscape architects who had arrived in the field via what was largely a horticultural or architectural background — had exacerbated the situation. To some of us, however, site sculpture was clearly art and subject to the sort of debate, criticism, and interpretation previously devoted mostly to works of painting, sculpture, and occasionally architecture. Even so, these highly promoted, site-specific creations were not the same as landscape architecture in that they didn't bear the same burdens and responsibilities, nor the great potential of landscape architecture when it solves and transcends its utilitarian purposes through artistic expression.

I consciously wrote the article in a manner parallel to those in which my colleagues at Harvard were presenting architecture at the time in an attempt to regain some of the high ground of previous eras and ambition in our field. As a person who is primarily a practitioner I was concerned that I not betray the sort of envy expressed by Steven Krog in his provocative articles a few years earlier — "Is it Art?" and "Creative Risk Taking" — albeit while being very sympathetic to what he was saying.[4] I hoped to encourage a deeper look into the potential of our medium for expression and content. The main points I tried to make could be summed up much as I wrote in the abstract that introduced the article.

In *Theory in Landscape Architecture,* Simon Swaffield categorizes me as one who argues that meaningful landscape design should express a distillation of the essential qualities of human experience paired with a consideration of nature. He is silent about, or chooses to ignore, however, something that I tried to make clear—and which Marc Treib noted in his riposte "Must Landscapes Mean?"—namely, that there are several ways by which landscapes come to possess meaning. Some of these have little if anything to do with nature or the intent of a designer; for example, the landscapes that comprise the sites of the nineteenth-century battlefield at Gettysburg, Pennsylvania, or that of the Sioux victory over the U.S. Cavalry at Little Big Horn in Wyoming. Their current cultural meaning derives solely from historic events, not the terrain itself or any designer's intent.

The bulk of my essay was devoted to considering some of those things that designers can do and what sort of devices can lead others —the public, visitors, whatever we call the users and perceivers of landscapes—to considerations, ideas, and thoughts about things not necessarily present on the site, whether they be about nature, the region, temporality, history, the human condition, or the medium of landscape. While I didn't make much of it at the time, it should be acknowledged that I was aware that designers can't make people think or feel anything. In the passage discussing rhetoric I tried to point out that one can proffer material from which others can then form impressions and thoughts of their own. As in any art, the skill with which one sets out the material—the selection and arrangement of the devices used to encourage others to think of particular (or general) things, to have both sensory experiences and discoveries of particular references, and the ability of an audience to be interested, to perceive and utilize such material—varies greatly with individuals and moments in time. Treib has questioned the efficacy or even the appropriateness of such endeavors, noting as others have, that our population today is so diverse, ethnically, culturally, and spiritually, that it may simply be futile to attempt to construct a landscape that can be "read" coherently for any meaning that its author(s) may wish to embody.

A few years later I published a long-delayed study on aspects of the English landscape.[5] One particular portion discussed at length eighteenth-century landscape gardens. An extended essay in the book discussed the development of Stourhead, one of the greatest achievements of the period, or for that matter, of all European gardens in the humanist tradition. The narrative, my reading of the site, was based upon extensive personal experience, and a survey of scholarship through the early 1980s. Since then various scholars have suggested other interpretations regarding some or all of the features I discussed.[6] None, however, has gone so far as to say that the men who created Stourhead were just messing about and that there wasn't intention in their work. Nor have any implied that there is no meaning to be found in the various pavilions, statues, inscriptions, the circuit of walks, views, and visual compositions. While I am convinced that this is one of the most literary or poetic of the gardens constructed in the English countryside of all times, I no longer believe (as I seem to have earlier) that it has a linear narrative such as one might find in traditional literature. I think it is laden with meaning, some accessible only to those who made it, some easily available to their contemporaries, and some for those of us familiar with their time and art. For many today, however, it almost certainly evokes things unintended by its authors regarding recreation, gardening, and class structures in the eighteenth century and today. For many I'm sure it is simply a huge and beautiful visual and sensory extravaganza.

Jane Gillette's critique of this essay (and her assertion, if I understand it) that landscapes can't really contain meaning at all, but that only written works, i.e., works composed of words, can do so, strikes me as simply untrue. Gillette used the word *gardens* not *landscape*, but it's the same quarrel for me. It is true that landscapes mean in a different way from literature. I made a particular point in the *Landscape Journal* article about this, quoting Nelson Goodman—

7 5 /

a colleague of mine at the time in the philosophy department at Harvard—with whom several of us frequently met over lunch to discuss this very problem. As he put it, "Architecture, non-objective painting and music have no subject. Their style cannot be a matter of how they say something, for they do not literally say anything; they do other things, they mean in other ways."[7] I was troubled then (and still am today) by linguistic analogies that several members of Harvard's Graduate School of Design and other architecture and landscape faculties used repeatedly. I disagreed with Goodman that landscape in the hands of designers can't have a "subject," even while agreeing that it wasn't the same as in language. Despite my own struggles to find a way to discuss the strategies and devices employed in landscape design that could engender meaning, I knew then (and now), and wrote matter of factly, "landscapes are not verbal constructions. [But] they can express certain things, can possess symbols, and refer to ideas, events, and objects extrinsic to their own elements and locus, and in certain circumstances can be didactic and/or highly poetic. How they do it is not well understood. That they do it is."[8]

It seems to me that there are many forms of knowing and understanding a variety of phenomena that are not linguistically based. One's body (or brain) has learned and knows the dimensions and position of furniture in our homes and the rhythm and proportions of innumerable stairways to the degree that we can traverse them in the dark without paying attention. Then there is music, that most abstract art. Despite volumes written on the subject, it (mostly) relates to itself and our knowledge of it is based neither upon verbal nor linguistic data or processes. My favorite example is that of a story told of Beethoven who, upon coming to the end of a performance of a new piano sonata in a patron's drawing room, was confronted by one of the guests who gushed how wonderful it was. But then she asked: "Please, could you tell me what it meant?" Silently returning to the keyboard he proceeded to play it through again. Upon completing the work he turned to her and said: "That, Madame, is what it means."

Another motive for writing "Form, Meaning, and Expression" was that I became aware of an enormous prejudice on the part of Harvard's central administration and numerous members of other schools toward the faculty and students in visual arts and the Graduate School of Design, largely because the basis of our work and its measures were neither linguistically nor mathematically determined. Some of the most brilliant designers in the nation (or world) came to teach and lecture at the school (as they also do at the University of Pennsylvania where I have taught for many years since), and their work has been considered extraordinarily beautiful, important as art, and a measure of the era's creativity—the stuff that embodies the aspirations and production of entire generations. Even so, we were not treated as intellectually equal to members of the humanities faculty, many of whom wrote articles for each other and small academic journals that in many cases are neither valued nor remembered today—and certainly can't be considered as critical elements of a lasting and meaningful cultural legacy.

I was convinced that designers knew things but that we knew them "in other ways" from our colleagues, as Goodman had remarked. Designers and artists know an awful lot—and not just skills or performance craft—but their knowledge all too often slips between words and is not easily discussed. Three of these topics in landscape of which we have knowledge, but cannot always articulate, are those of form, meaning, and expression. Despite their great interest to me I must set aside the discussion of form and expression for now, because they are huge topics, enormously important, and like meaning require extended discourse to treat them reasonably.

Just as there are levels of meaning and discourse in language, ranging from laundry lists to business letters, from narrative fiction to lyric poetry, so too are there levels of meaning in landscape. They range from the mundane to the profound whether they are attractive, disheveled, beautiful or not, small or large. One must acknowledge that much of the built world is composed of banal, background places that are at most utilitarian or instrumental. This is probably a very good thing. At best they are merely a setting for something, whether for parking automobiles or marking a location for a building and its address. They are not called to do or mean anything more than this. The suburbs comprise a landscape largely made of such stuff. There are also landscapes, like the Pennsylvania Turnpike, that are primarily infrastructure or systems with purpose and character that do not denote much beyond their own intentions. They can be handsome and offer visual experiences that are powerful and rich, such as those offered by the Blue Ridge Parkway. Along the way there can be places with particular references and meanings derived from cultural objects, events, or particular visions presented (the battle road between Lexington and Concord for example). But it is fair to say that most parkways and their environs do not mean much more than an attractive way to drive through a portion of mountains or countryside, allowing driver and passengers a continual visual experience of variety and beauty. And then there are landscapes we purposefully make to remind us of particular things.

Unfortunately, my earlier writing may have muddied the waters a bit on this subject. By 1980, when I began trying to write on this topic, nearly all of the literature on landscape history had been made by a generation of scholars trained as art historians in an era heavily influenced by the Warburg and Courtauld Institutes and several of its key individuals interested in Renaissance iconography. This was the lens I began with. Architectural history and criticism at the time — the late 1970s and early 1980s — was emerging from a period of influence by prominent neo-Marxists or sociologists, especially French structuralists and the Annales group of historians, social critics, and philosophers. Deconstruction and post-structuralist ideas were flooding into American academia in literature and the humanities. It was difficult to find a way to discuss meaning in landscape that didn't fall into one of these thickets — what else to call them, pools of thought, swamps? It would be a few years before John Dixon Hunt would consider the realm of user/visitor/public perception as a way to construe sense and meaning, multiple and contradictory as that may be. His writing, especially as recently summarized in *The Afterlife of Gardens*, is very much in line with the post-structural, post-modern dethroning of authorial mastery and control wherein the critic, reader, or others take control of meaning. There were also other sorts of attacks on artists and designers: "What do these idiot-savant authors and artists, Melville, Hawthorne, Wright, Olmsted, and the like, know?" It was for the critics to tell us, to become the new *über*-artists, using works of art and design as grist for their creations. At its best this stance leads to a diverse set of readings with widely ranging interpretations, often rich in their interplay. At worst it has become a thick lens through which it is often difficult to actually see or experience the work itself.

As I see it now, much of the latter twentieth-century work that interests me does not lend itself well to an analysis based upon iconographic models. At the same time the close reading one enjoys with poetry can only be applied to landscape with great care and subtle examination of the myriad elements and their relationships. Landscapes are made of many diverse phenomena—visual, aural, tactile, olfactory—that may trigger the recall of things from our own personal environmental history, which in turn combine with a world of information from our education and experience. For this reason there is no question in my mind that the art of landscape design—when it is an art—is possibly the most complex and sophisticated art we possess. That said, despite some of the remarkable minds that have considered the topic, our ability to adequately analyze and discuss the designed landscape and its meanings seems to be among our least successful endeavors. It is easy to attack most of the discussions regarding meaning in landscape: for no matter how right they may be, at heart they are fragile constructions—unlike their subject.

IN CLOSING

Some landscapes demand to be extraordinary, if for no other reason than to sustain the pressure of expectation that they be emotionally moving, disturbing, and assertive. One such project is the Memorial to the Murdered Jews of Europe in Berlin, engaging as it does background and foreground: ordinary and non-striving versus assertive, attention-getting elements [figure 1-10]. What, you may ask, does this landscape or its myriad parts mean? People come away with a variety of feelings, impressions, and interpretations, especially regarding the thousands of concrete objects that make up the "field"—in all of their cold weight—rather the opposite of our usual association with the word "field." While the elements of the memorial—erected on the very spot where the fatal apparatus of the Nazi regime was located—are stated and constant, each visitor will perceive and independently construct his or her own views, ideas, and attitudes to the place and interpret them accordingly. And while it is common knowledge that the memorial's underlying subject is death on an unprecedented and barely conceivable scale—a reminder for both those who lived through the period of atrocities and those who have entered the world thereafter—it leaves those constructions partly, maybe largely, up to the visitor. Nowhere are there inscriptions, legends, mottos, or figurative representations of any kind. In that way it differs strikingly from the work of Ian Hamilton Finlay at Stony Path in Scotland or Lawrence Halprin's Roosevelt Memorial in Washington, D.C. It is a landscape of concrete, granite, topography, and a few plants. The memorial is simply a landscape. The landscape is a memorial. It means a lot to me. What it means to other people I cannot say, but it must, of necessity, mean something.

> **meaningless** *adj. 1. Without meaning, significance, or value; purposeless; insignificant: a meaningless reply: a meaningless existence."*[9]

NOTES

1 *The Random House Dictionary of the English Language*, New York, 1966, p. 888.

2 Laurie Olin, "Form, Meaning, and Expression in Landscape Architecture," *Landscape Journal*, Number 2, 1988, pp. 149–168.

3 This statement was written by my partner, Robert Hanna, ten years earlier, in 1977. This later philosophical difference became a deep source of tension between us, contributing in part to our eventual breakup.

4 Steven Krog, "Is It Art?" *Landscape Architecture*, May 1981, pp. 373–376; "Creative Risk Taking," *Landscape Architecture*, March 1983, pp. 70–76.

5 Laurie Olin, *Across the Open Field*, Philadelphia: University of Pennsylvania Press, 2000, especially pp. 257–276.

6 Most notably Malcolm Kelsall, who in "The Iconography of Stourhead," *Journal of the Warburg and Courtauld Institutes*, 1983, pp. 133–143, dismisses aspects of Kenneth Woodbridge's thought that had influenced me considerably. See John Dixon Hunt, "Stourhead Revisited and the Pursuit of Meaning in Gardens," *Studies in the History of Gardens and Designed Landscapes*, October–December 2006, pp. 328–341.

7 Nelson Goodman, *Ways of Worldmaking*, Cambridge, MA: Hackett Publishing, 1978, p. 23.

8 Olin, "Form, Meaning, and Expression," p. 158.

9 *The Random House Dictionary of the English Language*, New York, 1966, p. 888.

2.

Must Landscapes Mean?

Approaches to

Significance

in Recent Landscape

Architecture

Marc Treib   [1995]

I.

During the last decade, the amount of writing purporting to address meaning in landscape design has grown impressively.[1] Landscape architects now write of their attempts to imbue designs with significance by referring to such conditions as existing natural forms or to the historic aspects of the site. Cultural geographers, calling upon a collective body of study that now extends back well over half a century, interpret ordinary landscapes by first looking at the world around them; in their eyes, meaning congeals in setting, dwelling, and use—and not alone from the designer's intention.[2] Historians of gardens and landscape architecture tell us of those makers of places past who tried earnestly to create landscapes in which meaning would be evident and understood. At times relying on iconography and inscription, the creators of these gardens and parks sought to convey to the visitor a mental as well as a sensual impression. Within the garden confines, the visitor would take

2-1

ISAMU NOGUCHI, *CALIFORNIA SCENARIO*, COSTA MESA, CALIFORNIA, 1984.

[MARC TREIB]

pause and perhaps ponder the meaning of existence, or at least his or her part of it. Since the visitor, owner, and maker tended to share class and culture, intelligible communication was feasible.

These are only a few examples of the interests that have surfaced in the last decade and that have filled the pages of numerous publications. Principal among them, *The Meanings of Gardens*, edited by Mark Francis and Randolph Hester, Jr., in 1990 collected a series of essays that ranged in topic from religion to pop culture, from sex to pets, and geographically from Israel to Norway.[3] In the book, authors drawn from diverse disciplines questioned the significance of the landscapes we create; there were no generic conclusions although the essays were somewhat neatly arranged under the headings of idea, place, and action. In a 1988 essay titled "From Sacred Grove to Disney World," Robert Riley also tracked the search for meaning—and its removal over time—and concluded: "Gardens have been a locus of meaning in many cultures, but not in modern America."[4]

What are we to make of these renewed efforts to discern meaning in landscapes? Is it really possible to build into landscape architecture a semantic dimension that communicates the maker's intention to the inhabitant? If so, by what means? In addition, *should* we try to reveal meaning in environments, and if so, why? Where does the audience enter the process? Admittedly, this is notoriously treacherous territory and every author begins—and often ends—by hedging his or her bets. Laurie Olin stressed the "daunting" task of defining meaning and suggested that there were two broad categories in which the term was positioned. The first he termed "natural" or "evolutionary": "Generally these relate to aspects of the landscape as a setting for society and have been developed as a reflection or expression of hopes and fears for survival and perpetuation."[5] More simply stated, significance accrues through use and custom. Olin's second category, and the arena in which most designers operate, concerned synthetic

84 / MARC TREIB / MUST LANDSCAPES MEAN?

or invented meanings, and it is these to which he devotes most of his essay and criticism.[6] My own effort will probably differ only slightly from that of almost every previous writer in that I will attempt to discuss the question of significance without precisely defining it.[7] To some degree this lacuna is problematic; in other ways it is may not be so troublesome.[8] I'd like to think that we can discuss the meaning of meaning in landscape without a definition applicable to all landscape circumstances. Or, at least I will operate under that premise. Surely we can establish a broad theater in which meaning is taken simply as an integral aspect of human lives, beyond any basic attachment to the land through familiarity. Meaning thus comprises ethics, values, history, affect—all of them taken singly or as a group.

We could first try to establish *why* the pursuit of meaning has resurfaced at the close of the twentieth century. One reason might be the rejection of history, and all the baggage it carried, by those formulating a modern(ist) American landscape design in the late 1930s. Unlike their European colleagues, who continually confronted history in the world around them, American designers often started with a relatively clean slate. James Rose and Garrett Eckbo, among other writers, aggressively challenged the value of history used as a lexicon of styles or typologies to be unquestioningly applied to modern problems and projects. Like their architectural contemporaries, they looked forward to solving problems of open space and form, and not backwards to any book of given solutions. The received body of historical landscape architecture was taken as meaningless because its significance belonged to other places and other times.[9]

Rose, in all probability borrowing from the Canadian/Englishman Christopher Tunnard, argued for what he termed a "structural" use of plants: vegetation selected for a given climatic zone, but configured to create spaces to be used from within rather than to be viewed from without.[10] A continuing theme in Eckbo's writings well into the

1950s was the condemnation of the axis, which he claimed had "run out of gas in the 17th century."[11] Like Rose, Eckbo envisioned an enriched landscape configured for use, rather than one restricted to a linear spatial structure based on formal concerns alone.

There was little or no discussion of meaning in these writings, as there was—quite remarkably—no argument for any specific vocabulary. Significance derived from forms and spaces appropriate to their use and times; meaning was a by-product, or so the text implied. Although the zigzag was a popular feature in the gardens of Eckbo and Thomas Church, and the biomorphism of Jean Arp and Isamu Noguchi informed much postwar California garden design, no published texts connected these idioms with either modern art or the modern era—or argued for their significance.[12] In fact, very little was written specifically about syntax—that is, the relationship between the elements —much less about semantic production.

Landscape writings of the period paralleled—almost always with a bit of time lag—discourse on modern architecture. Sigfried Giedion, the central theorist for what came to be termed the International Style, rationalized the new architectural vocabulary by setting it against spatially vital architectures past.[13] The modernist art critic Clement Greenberg saw painting first and foremost as marks upon a canvas and found its the culmination in non-objective works that stressed the flatness of the canvas; Gideon saw in modernist building the culmination of architecture as space.[14] In so doing, he actually recast history to accord with a twentieth-century vantage point. In anthropological terms, he was etic rather than emic, that is, looking at the subject from beyond its cultural limits rather than on its own terms. While a vast repertoire of Western architecture had accumulated over time, to Gideon its quest had ultimately been spatial rather than stylistic, and as such it reached fruition in the modern era. Because he found space more central to architecture than either iconography or human affect, Gideon was more focused on architectonics (i.e., on architectural syntax) than on semantics. Or perhaps he regarded significance and the means of spatial production as synonymous. Garrett Eckbo's *Landscape for Living* of 1950 provided the modernist argument with its text and laid out the concerns and parameters for modern landscape architecture.[15] More fully developed in breadth and depth than earlier writings by either Tunnard or Rose, Eckbo's writing reinforced the need for reflecting time and place and human presence in landscape architecture: but there was no discussion of what it meant.

In many ways, the next major ideological and highly polemical tract was Ian McHarg's *Design with Nature*, published in 1969. Focused on the evolving study of natural ecology and rooted in landscape management, McHarg cited the natural world as the only viable source of landscape design. His text provided landscape architects with sufficient moral grounds for almost completely avoiding decisions of design—if design is taken as the conscious shaping of landscape beyond its stewardship. No talk of meaning here, only of natural processes and a moral imperative.[16] Laurie Olin, among others, has pointed out that design decisions normally derive from a greater complexity of factors than those of ecology alone, among them social and cultural issues including aesthetics, and cautions: "[T]his chilling, close-minded stance of moral certitude is hostile to the vast body of work produced through history, castigating it as 'formal' and as representing the dominance of humans over nature."[17] McHarg mixed science with evangelism—a sort of Eco-Fundamentalism as it is sarcastically known by some parties— taking no prisoners and allowing no quarter.

The McHargian view was focused to the point of being exclusive, conflating two rather different arenas of landscape intervention/ modulation as if they were one.[18] To manage a region without thorough "scientific" investigation and analysis would be fatuous, if not dangerous. Viable design begins with purposeful study and analysis. But the planning process rarely requires the active form-making that is central to landscape architecture. Reams of analysis and overlays will establish the parameters for making a garden for a suburban backyard, but they will hardly provide the design. McHarg's method insinuated that if the process was morally and analytically correct, the form would be good, almost as if an aesthetic automatically resulted from objective study. Presumably, meaning would accompany the resulting landscape.

The 1960s and 1970s were dominated by attempts to rationalize the practices of architecture and landscape architecture, favoring social utility over the pursuit of form and/or significance. By the end of the decade, however, the limits to this way of thinking, coupled with an emerging desire by younger landscape architects to again become visible, began to generate a reaction to the anti-aesthetic and anti-semantic climates of the preceding decade.

Admittedly, this is a cursory explanation of a professional condition that derived from a complex series of interrelated factors. Landscape architecture is, after all, a part of a cultural, technical, and social milieu and as such is informed by a multitude of factors and considerations. But…

II.

During the 1980s, declarations of meaning began to accompany the published photos and drawings of landscape designs. At conferences, landscape architects described their intentions, their sources, and what they believed their designs signified. Some designers merely claimed they were once again touching base with the vernacular matrix in which High Style design was embedded. Martha Schwartz, for example, re-examined the materials of the ordinary landscape and the typologies of the small private garden and the shopping center. George Hargreaves spoke of a perceptually complex space at the 1984 Harlequin Plaza in Inglewood, Colorado, although he shied away from making direct claims about its meaning(s) [see figure 1-2]. The emerging generation of designers displayed a new interest in making form; and many of them claimed that these new forms would be meaningful. Landscape architecture from these two decades might be assigned to one or more of five roughly framed approaches and by extension, to a striving for significance: the Neo-Archaic, the Genius of the Place, the Zeitgeist, the Vernacular Landscape, and the Didactic.

A sort of primitivism constituted one attempt to retrieve what had been lost at some unspecified point along the way to modernity. Borrowing from schools of art that ranged from the body works of Ana Mendieta to the stone markings of Richard Long to the theories of entropy proffered by Robert Smithson, landscape architects began to re-configure the land in a manner we could term *Neo-Archaic*. Whether the landscape architects referred directly to neolithic sources, or only to the sculptors who had drawn upon them, is impossible to determine. Perhaps they tapped both resources. But in neighborhood playgrounds and in suburban office parks, one began to encounter hills coiled with spiral paths, cuts in the earth aligned with the rising or setting sun (or the summer solstice), circles of broken stone, and clusters of sacred groves. Granite stelae evoking the stone circles of ancient Scandinavia—or was that Easter Island or England's Salisbury Plain?—appeared in backyards and plazas. Myriad versions of Jai Singh's eighteenth-century astronomical observatories at Delhi and Jaipur popped up like mushrooms, including one reinterpretation in a fine garden by the master Isamu Noguchi [figure 2-1].[19] One can almost hear designers saying, *sotto voce*: "If they meant something in the past (of course, we have to like them as forms…), then they will mean something again to us today." Gary Dwyer's proposal to link the two sides of the San Andreas Fault in California with crisscrossed topographic band-aids curiously developed from the Ogham writing of the Celts is extreme to be sure—and rather difficult to support with rational argument—but it was not at all bizarre in the context of contemporary projects.[20] As the landscape historian Catherine Howett once aptly phrased it: "By the early 1980s, every landscape-architecture student project had been equinoxed to death."[21]

If archaicism was one school of semantic creation, the worship of the *Genius of the Place* marked a second. Alexander Pope had enjoined Lord Burlington to consult the spirit of the place as a means of rooting landscape design in a particular locale. A garden was not a universal concept to be applied without inflection upon all sites. Instead, the garden revealed the particularities of its place as well as the profundity of the garden's idea. Long driven underground by the onslaught of urbanity, suburbanity, and modern technology, the genius was a bit hesitant to re-emerge into the twentieth-century sunlight and as a result, came out squinting. A renewed cult figure, the genius—or what was left of him or her—could be consulted in many places in only a desultory way since "the place" had been so disturbed by centuries of industrial and residential development. While writers such as Christian Norberg-Schulz based their discussion of the genius of the place in the phenomenology of Maurice Merleau-Ponty and others decried the rise of an endemic placelessness, designers often adopted superficial approaches to connect human inhabitants and their landscape setting.[22]

History became an image to be dusted off and applied to any current proposal as a means of validation. In a glance over the shoulder of history, the tiny urban park was planted with prairie grass to show what vegetation had once thrived there. Like the caged animal in the zoo, however, an urban prairie is hardly a prairie at all—it is an urban garden planted with grass left unmown and little else. At best, it has been reduced to a sign for what had been. Since the frame for reading—that is to say its context—had been so drastically altered, the design is not easily understood by contemporary citizens as a reference to the past. The grass that so magnificently sheathed the prairie has been reduced from an inherent and meaningful component of early settlement to a design, or at best a museological, feature. Meaning arrives on the face of a plastic or metal plaque that credits the designer, the sponsoring body (usually a benevolent foundation for Green America), and of course, the mayor in office at the time. Still, most passersby wonder quietly to themselves: "When are they going to cut that lawn? I'm sure there are rats and Lord knows what else living in it. And they should water it; it looks dead."[23]

The presence of the genius is a bit more obvious in undisturbed land, but there is precious little of that around these days, as s/he has hardly been left unaffected by changes in atmosphere and climate. Still, the genius provides major support for landscape design and its rationalization today. Technically, studies of vegetation, hydrology, soil conditions, and the like are indeed the basis of design; but do these suggest a significant form for the design? If there is a stand of oaks, do you plant more oaks? Or should the stand be complemented by another species that even to the untrained eye appears to be foreign to the site?[24] So much of landscape architecture in the past has been created to *overcome* what the genius of the place offered the "unimproved" land—for example, by bringing water to the desert or by constructing conditioned enclosures to grow oranges in colder climates —that it is obvious that his/her ambiguous advice can be interpreted rather freely. In instances such as the Patio of the Oranges in Seville the human contrivance of irrigation was elevated to an art form, creating a garden of exceptional pleasure, refinement, and tranquility. Needless to say, this beautiful and beautifully verdant forecourt was not conceived as a xeriscape that relied upon native plants; admittedly, it was collective and religious, rather than an anonymous private, vernacular garden. But this courtyard—like other pieces of greenery and water in arid climates—nevertheless illustrates that while one should consult Genius & Company, one needn't accept the advice in precisely the manner it was given. Like any consultation, the information must be evaluated and some decisions need to be made, including those of form [figure 2-2].

Buried within this approach to shaping the landscape is the belief that reflecting a pre-existing condition creates a design more meaningful to the inhabitants. Why so? Many of these inhabitants weren't present on the planet at the time the land was pristine. I recently attended a project presentation that informed those gathered that as the principal concept for a natural preserve the designers and clients had recently restored the historical ecology in its original pattern. That they had also created a pond where none had existed—assumedly as much for the visitors as for the birds that were to be lured to this reserve—was passed over without question. It is difficult to fault the good intentions of restoring disturbed wetlands. But why "restore" the original pattern when, in fact, the reserve today serves equally for human recreation and open-space preservation? Is it because the "natural" pattern, masquerading as nature, is less open to question by client or visitor alike? Or could it be that the designers, somewhat defensively, do not believe they can improve upon the natural pattern to bring the landscape into greater accord with the new uses and the drift of the times? Or is it a conscious or unconscious harking back to received picturesque values? Does the genius really grant significance, or does he or she just point out the easiest path to follow—what in the zoological world is called a "target of opportunity"? [This will be discussed further in Part III below.]

2-2

COURTYARD OF
THE ORANGES,
SEVILLE, SPAIN, 16th C+.
[MARC TREIB]

Approach number three borrows from related disciplines, which suggests a belief in the *Zeitgeist* (i.e., "the spirit of the times") as a determining force for any aspect of contemporary culture. If artists, and the battery of cultural critics that support and explain their work, have produced a body of work deemed illustrative of the spirit of our times, then landscapes designed with contemporary art-like elements must share that significance. Such an approach intersects at times with the Neo-Archaic, particularly in recent years when a new regard for prehistory has informed at least one major strain of art making.[25]

The boulders that comprise Peter Walker's 1984 Tanner Fountain at Harvard bear a striking resemblance to those Carl Andre had neatly arranged in his *Stone Field Sculpture* in Hartford some seven years earlier [see figure 4-2, figure 2-3]. Andre, in spite of ultra-minimalist proclivities, had actually consulted the Genius in creating the work, choosing a range of stone types native to the surrounding area as the basic material of the installation. (Because the rocks had been removed from their native context, however, the populace required a written or verbal explanation to inform them of the fact.) Walker's stones, in contrast, are all more or less the same size and type, and their circular configuration—like certain elements of his later IBM Solana, Texas, campus—also cite rather directly the work of sculptor Richard Long. Certainly an aesthetic transformation has been employed; neither the fountain nor courtyard design in any way constitutes a plagiarized form. But much of their novelty and appeal— at least at the date of their initiation—derives from their seeming correlation with art forms of the times. From sculpture, the designer receives both the instigation of ideas and, to some degree, of validation. Landscape architecture becomes in the process a part of the ethos of the era, and its own identity as

2-3

CARL ANDRE,
STONE FIELD SCULPTURE,
HARTFORD, CONNECTICUT,
1977.
[MARC TREIB]

an art is confirmed. This is not a bad practice as it acknowledges the importance of regarding landscape architecture as a cultural as well as environmental practice.

Perhaps the most prominent recent example of the Zeitgeist approach is the 1988 Parc de la Villette in Paris, won in competition by Bernard Tschumi. Bounded on one edge by the Périphérique [ring road], described by the architectural historian Norma Evenson as the concrete moat that surrounds Paris, the site was offered little by the Genius Loci, and a Didactic [see below] approach would have demanded a strong evocation of the site's history or even the re-institution of the animal slaughter that once transpired on the site.[26] Instead, Tschumi used notions of cinematic sequence, events, and post-structural theories concerning the fragmentation of postmodern culture as sources for the park's design. The "outmoded" concept of park was supposedly dissolved by these new ideas, instead producing a design that effaced the boundary between city and park and eliminated the hard line between built and green zones.

The drawings used to explain the competition design were brilliantly conceived and included an exploded axonometric view that masterfully conveyed the design concept of point, line, and surface—a visual equivalent of a "sound-bite." Unfortunately, parks are rarely seen from the air and even less frequently as exploded axonometrics. In fact, as a totality, the non-composition recalls too closely the bland and amorphous open spaces of Paris's *grands ensembles* (housing projects) of the 1950s and 1960s [figure 2-4]. La Villette's red follies, while intriguing as investigations of architectural form, do little to energize the park's sensual appeal beyond the visual. Ultimately there is precious little of genuine, that is to say *experiential*, interest as landscape architecture on the site. Basically, the landscape comprises some lawn and some rows of trees.[27] The ideas used to

2-4

BERNARD TSCHUMI,
PARC DE LA VILLETTE,
PARIS, 1988+.
[MARC TREIB]

conceive the park are rich and evocative; the experience on site is limited and somewhat spatially uninteresting, however. At what point does concept end and experience begin? Is an intriguing concept sufficient to create meaning in the minds of the beholders? What of the beholder not privy to the designer's convoluted explanation? The Parc de la Villette illustrates the problems that plague borrowing parallel ideas or forms from other disciplines and the distortion that often accompanies translation. In this particular Parisian example, what has been written about the project is far more intriguing that what one encounters on site.[28] The ultimate success or failure of such landscape designs does not ultimately derive from their intellectual origins but whether or not they "work" on their own merits as places and landscapes, without recourse to jargon and verbal explanations. One might also ask in the end: What pleasure do they provide?

Like architects such as Robert Venturi and Frank Gehry, landscape architects such as Martha Schwartz also look at the *Vernacular Landscape*. This is a hip glance at the Genius of the Place, of course, but the genius is culturalized and the selections suave. The vernacular is a rich source of materials and forms; after all, it constitutes the "real" world in which we dwell. But just as the meanings of historical landscapes are affected by re-framing, the vernacular landscape is inevitably transformed when borrowed by design professionals. And when vernacular elements reappear in High Style projects, taken semantically they have virtually nothing in common with their sources. They have been re-framed and reconstituted. Designers treat the vernacular environment as a quarry for raw materials to be reconfigured and thus transfigured. The unselfconsciousness, the appropriate sense of the makeshift, and the accepted transience of vernacular building normally disappear along the way.[29] A glass gazing ball optically enlarges the confines of a small

2-5

MARTHA SCHWARTZ, CENTER FOR INNOVATIVE TECHNOLOGY, HERNDON, VIRGINIA, 1988. [MARC TREIB]

backyard private garden while serving as a sign of neighborly propriety. When it is extracted from the back yard, repeated at length, and arranged in a grid, however, only the basic reflective properties remain unaffected [figure 2-5]. Similarly, a concrete frog accompanying a cement deer and perhaps a gnome are tender companions in an intimate garden setting. Multiplied by the hundreds and painted gold, they are no longer the common vernacular element they once were, but fodder for High Style designers [see figure 3-4]. This is not to say they possess no merit of their own, they most certainly do; but the meaning is no longer vernacular. Like fine wine, significance doesn't travel very well, and wine *does* differ from grape juice.

The fourth approach to "constructed meaning" goes down the *Didactic* path. This is the one I have found most appealing, and one that has formed the only more-or-less stable leg of our own projects. In fact, it was a friend's observation while examining a current project that made me realize that much of what we do represents a somewhat desperate search for meaning in the landscape.[30] The Didactic approach dictates that forms should tell us—in fact instruct us—about the natural workings or history of the place. This is related—as all the approaches are to some degree—to the Genius Loci school but the Didactic is usually more overt in its intentions. Not only should we consult the Genius about its basis, but our resultant project should render an exegesis on what the Genius told us.[31]

Curiously, we often try to restore what has been previously destroyed. Perhaps a stream long culverted and buried is restored to its "original" state (of course, it really isn't—everything has changed around it). One of the rules formulated by Joel Garreau in *Edge City* is that one names a place for the features that have been destroyed to make room for the new development.[32] Shady Hills Estates commemorates the trees that were cut to build the houses, and the natural undulations that were flattened to make construction less challenging;

and incidentally, the houses are small tract houses and hardly estates. But like the photo caption, the name of the development directs our reading of the place and asks us to complete what is missing in the picture. A design didactically conceived, like the photo caption, is both informative—possibly normative—and certainly directive. The "factual" base is intended to validate the designer's work.

A Didactic landscape is supposedly an aesthetic textbook on natural or, in some cases, urban processes. Alexandre Chemetoff's sunken bamboo garden at La Villette purposely allowed the elements of urban infrastructure to remain, reminding the visitor that this small green respite was actually but a fragment of an urban agglomeration that required massive amounts of servicing to exist [see figure 4-3]. Water mains, sewer pipes, and electrical ducts crisscross the site; the retaining walls are constructed of pre-cast concrete elements commonly used to support the walls of adjacent sites during excavation for new construction. The landscape architect did not leave these elements of infrastructure untouched, however; the scheme itself developed as a give-and-take between the didactic exposure of services and its aesthetic complement in wispy green and gold foliage. Sculptors —who almost by definition are allowed to consider the aesthetic parameter in isolation—have also created places structured on the Didactic dimension. At the National Oceanographic and Atmospheric Administration in Seattle, for example, Douglas Hollis's *A Sound Garden* (1983) captured the wind to activate an environmental organ; the vanes aligning the field of erect pipes into the gusts added a visual signal of wind direction [figure 2-6]. Here the presence of the wind received both aural and visual expression.

In these two instances, the work of landscape art addressed either natural or urban process with an assumption—which I have since come to suspect—that designs revealing these processes are both more viable and more meaningful. I don't think the answer is quite that simple.

Didactic thinking supplies a good point of departure for the work, but the success of the place ultimately hinges on the skill and care invested in the design and on what it offers the visitor. Didacticism per se is not enough. (In these two instances the final success of the resulting works—and I do regard them as successful—did not depend on their Didactic aspects alone, but a host of factors that does not exclude siting, materials, aesthetics, and sophistication.)

And then there is the *Theme Garden*. It is curious to me how many people deride the world's Disneylands and other theme parks and then propose Theme Gardens. A theme, in this context, constitutes a perceptually apparent idea used to fashion the garden's form. Roses, Mother Goose, the color yellow, or even electric light could all be used as themes, and I imagine all of them have been used as such somewhere at some time. One could argue that the gamut of themes deriving from horticultural or environmental ideas or cultural borrowings are inherently more genuine than the contrived imagery of a theme park created in plaster or plastic, but they are themes nonetheless.[33]

A theme, it must be admitted, is not necessarily an argument for significance, but there is an underlying assertion of validity that accompanies any obvious concept. Even today, the landscape professional can accept a Chinese garden, for example that by Fletcher Steele at Naumkeag or the copper tents at Frederik Magnus Piper's eighteenth-century Haga Park in Stockholm [figure 2-7]. Perhaps we use the word "charming" rather than "beautiful" to qualify them. If well done, in fact, the effect of the pavilion or cultural borrowing is far greater than its semantic theme. It can be pleasant, calming, restful, stimulating, in its own right; that is, it can affect us. Which tells us something about the experiential dimensions of the garden.

2-6

DOUGLAS HOLLIS,
A SOUND GARDEN,
NATIONAL OCEANIC
AND ATMOSPHERIC
ADMINISTRATION,
SEATTLE, WASHINGTON,
1983.
[MARC TREIB]

The white garden at Sissinghurst is a well-known example of color used as a subject, but the themed approach is widespread in time and place. The recently opened Parc André Citroën in Paris includes "black" and "white" gardens, although in both gardens green seems to be the predominant color. One could argue that restriction to a single color suggests a poverty of horticultural invention or an overly zealous pursuit of minimalism. It can also, of course, create a garden of stunning beauty, employing incredible horticultural acrobatics and subtle chromatic mixtures even within a single color range.

Gilles Clément, the landscape architect responsible for a considerable section of the park, has also applied his idea of a "garden in movement" to one of its riverside zones [figure 2-8]. Here a score of wildflowers and grasses has been planted with little regard as to which will survive or where. Paths through these meadows will be determined by human movement rather than by formal design; the paths will fix the traces of occupation and use. This Darwinian approach to park design—which joins the Didactic to the Theme with instructive aesthetic consequences—addresses both the social issues brought to the fore in the 1960s and aspects of urban ecology. While these parts of the park will evolve in terms of horticultural species— and over time run the risk of looking like a vacant lot—they suggest the human presence only through a relatively few wooden seating platforms raised slightly above the ground. The idea of replicating evolution to establish an appropriate urban landscape is engaging, although the form may not be attractive at all times. But do they mean anything to anyone today?[34]

2-7

FLETCHER STEELE,
CHINESE GARDEN,
NAUMKEAG,
STOCKBRIDGE,
MASSACHUSETTS;
1937; 1955.
[MARC TREIB]

III.

Is it really possible to imbue a place with meaning from the outset? It would seem that history tells us yes, if the users possess sufficient experience in common. For one, significance is culturally circumscribed and, ultimately, personally determined.[35] If we examine a Chinese poem executed in ink on silk, as non-readers of the Chinese language we are denied access to the poem's linguistic dimension. Should we be uninitiated into Chinese calligraphy and the propriety and taste conveyed by the chosen style, the marks will have even less meaning to us. Should we so choose, we can always appreciate the work solely on its formal dimensions, of course, as fluid black marks on a white ground. It is obvious, however, that possessing linguistic abilities in Chinese would enrich both our understanding and our pleasure: the two-dimensional writing on the page would acquire multiple semantic dimensions.

The same is true of gardens. The uninitiated may or may not appreciate a dry "Zen" garden for its formal properties alone, for the pattern of its raked sand and the composition of its rocks; but the cultural meanings of the garden will remain communicated imperfectly at best. The absence of many of the elements that say "garden" to members of foreign cultures denies access to meaning just as the religious proscriptions deny physical access into the space.[36]

The Japanese dry garden provides a valuable case study for considering the construction of meaning. Japan's centuries of cultural homogeneity fostered an attitude towards simplicity as the compression of complexity (rather than its reduction or elimination, as it has been in the West). One could say, with perhaps only a little exaggeration, that until relatively recently a Japanese of a certain class / educational level could understand the intentions behind the making of the garden. He or she could appreciate

2-8

GILLES CLÉMENT,
LE JARDIN EN MOUVEMENT,
PARC ANDRÉ CITROËN,
PARIS, FRANCE, 1993.
[MARC TREIB]

the framing of the space; the non-geometric order within the enclosure; the quality of the rocks and their arrangement; the shaping of bushes; the almost complete absence of brilliantly flowering species. Unless familiar with Zen doctrine, however, the site's significance as an embodiment of religious belief, and possibly as intended by the garden maker, would remain beyond comprehension. And since Zen reflects continually back on the self for understanding and ultimately enlightenment, there is an implicit denial of meaning within the landscape itself. Instead, the garden as well as its care may stimulate individual contemplation; it can be seen as a vehicle for understanding the self rather than the place. The meaning of the garden is non-meaning. In Zen belief, the place bears no meaning per se, but it can perhaps evoke a call for meaning within the individual.

Allusions to worlds beyond the garden in place and time have appeared with some regularity in the polite traditions of landscape design in both East and West.[37] Replicas or recollections of Roman temples often appeared in the English landscape garden, for example. At Katsura Rikyu in Kyoto a small spit of water-worn stones was intended to cast the visitor's musings toward the peninsula of Amano-hashidate, long regarded as one of Japan's most outstanding shoreline landscapes [figure 2-9]. The shorn bamboo-covered slope at Koraku-en in today's Tokyo, on the other hand, specifically invoked the Mountain of the Chinese Immortals. Unlike the abstract Zen landscapes that were intended to summon a multitude of (ultimately personal) interpretations and associations, the aristocratic villa gardens often established intimations of legend and land. Meaning accrued from allusions to real or mythic geography beyond the garden's limits.

John Dixon Hunt has cogently argued that the world of the English landscape garden, like many garden traditions before it, was a coherent system of

2-9

KATSURA RIKYU,
AMA-NO-HASHIDATE
PENINSULA,
KYOTO, JAPAN,
17th C.
[MARC TREIB]

signs devised to be legible to both maker and visitor.[38] Here the signs were made tangible: a temple based on a familiar Roman predecessor; a vale with mythological reference; an architectonic emblem of Englishness. References could be manifest in a landscape feature, a structure, or even a written inscription to reduce ambiguity. Although falling under the common heading of signification, they actually concern two structures of meaning, differentiated in time. The first regarded the production of meaning used at the moment of the garden's creation and its effect(iveness) on the visitor. The second concerned the greater orbit of meaning that is part of the garden as an institution and a semiotic constellation. "Gardens, too, mean rather than are," claims this garden historian. "Their various signs are constituted of all the elements that compose them—elements of technical human intervention like terraces or the shape of flower-beds, elements of nature like water and trees—but they are nonetheless signs, to be read by outsiders in time and space for what they tell of a certain society."[39] Hunt also states—at first seemingly in contradiction with what he has written earlier in the essay—that even the most specific of references (probably textual ones) become timeworn and lose their significance: "Castle Howard and Rousham provide excellent examples of garden experience we have totally lost. We no longer see a representation of English landscape; we just see it."[40]

Any symbolic system demands education for comprehending both the medium and the message. One might understand, for example, that Diana was the goddess of the chase and even know of her association with the moon, but still might have absolutely no idea why her likeness stands in the garden. Were we unaware of Louis XIV's self-association with the sun, would we not believe Versailles to be a glorious homage to cloudy France's sunshine lost or to Apollo himself? We may have lost the ability to read some or all of the original intentions, but we can still decipher the original garden elements on our own contemporary terms. That these two worlds of meaning mutate over time suggests that meaning is indeed dynamic and ever-changing.[41] It also suggests that the meaning with which the designer believes he or she is investing the garden may have only minimal impact in the beginning, and even less in years to come.[42] On the other hand, he or she does have power over the artifact and its immediate effect on the senses —and its *potential* to mean.

Communication theory tells us that the two parties in conversation must share a common semantic channel or there will be no real interchange, no communication. Can the garden operate as such a channel and does the designer possess the power to create a significant landscape, especially given the multitude of communication channels in today's pluralistic world? When a society is relatively homogenized, the task is far easier because the designer shares the values and belief system of the people. Folk cultures produce places that are almost immediately communicative, and communicative over long periods. Because their connections between form and intention are understood within the culture and evolve only slowly over time, it is possible for the makers, the people, and the meaning of place to remain in contact.[43]

The Woodland Cemetery outside Stockholm, designed between 1915 and 1940 by Gunnar Asplund and Sigurd Lewerentz, tapped into the religious and value systems of the Swedish Lutheran congregants. This landscape of remembrance has remained meaningful to its parishioners, and appreciated by them, from the time of its realization. The triumph of the cemetery lies not only in its magnificent joining of architecture and landscape, and the modulated juncture of re-formed land with the existing pine forest, but also in its ability to conjure a sense of sanctity without relying on overt Christian iconography. Perhaps the power of this funereal landscape ultimately derives from an almost animistic feeling of pre-Christianity that addresses the forest, the land, and the heavens as a primeval setting [figure 2-10]. Perhaps the design also tapped into something basic to Swedish religion and culture. It might still be possible to create a landscape equally attuned to its time and place today, when Swedish society is far more diverse. But it would be far more difficult to devise the forms and symbols that would resonate within the contemporary Swedish population in quite the same way.[44] Not that it was ever easy; but it was certainly easier earlier in the century. The communication channels are no longer so few, nor are the elements of the Swedish landscape so simple.

To summarize:

Can a (landscape) designer help make a significant place? Yes.

Can a (landscape) designer design significance into the place at the time of its realization? No, or let's say, no longer in most places.

When a society was homogenous and shared a common system of belief, when the symbolic system was endemic, when the makers of places operated unselfconsciously fully within the culture, it was possible.[45] But even then, meaning was enriched through habit and the passage of time. Given the fragmentation of contemporary American society, and especially with its current emphasis on difference, the concord necessary for instant meaning is—to say the least—deficient.

Since a commissioning body might include meaningfulness as a part of its brief, why commission a (landscape) designer?

Of course, there are the pragmatic aspects of design that can best be addressed by those with an education, technical knowledge, and experience. One also hopes that the landscape architect possesses equal skill in understanding people and culture as well as horticulture and form. Creating significant landscapes remains a quest of the profession, as well

2-10

GUNNAR ASPLUND AND SIGURD LEWERENTZ, WOODLAND CEMETERY, ENSKEDE, SWEDEN, 1915–1940.

[MARC TREIB]

it should. But calling attention to Celtic inscriptions, solar alignments, the spirit of the place, the zeitgeist, the vernacular landscape, or even a didactic lesson in the derivation of form does not create meaning. Providing signifiers is not the same as creating significance, although it may be one point along the path. To my mind significance ultimately lies with the beholder and not in the place. Meaning accrues over time; like respect, it is earned, it is not granted. While the designer yearns to establish a landscape that will acquire significance, pat symbols alone do not transform syntax into semantics, that is, tectonics into meaning.[46]

Familiarity and affect are not quite the same as significance although they can serve as vehicles for its creation. To recall the site of one's first camping trip, or the park where the football championship was won, or even the flowers of one's family home ground establishes associations among place, act, and form that cohere in landscape meaning. If these places were designed by landscape architects, all well and good. Meaning condenses at the intersection of people and place, and not alone in the form the designer's idea takes.

The design itself constitutes a filter that creates the difference between what the designer intends and what the visitor experiences. This is the difference between the intended perception and the perceived intention. Differences in culture, in education, in life experience, in our experience of nature will all modify our perception of the work of landscape architecture. While this transaction between people and place is never completely symmetrical, we *can* circumscribe the range of possible reactions to a designed place. We cannot make that place mean, but we can hopefully instigate reactions to the place that will fall within the desired confines of happiness, gloom, joy, contemplation, or delight. This range of possible reactions, while tempered by cultural norms and personal experience, is still physiologically dependent on the human body. The limits of thermal comforts, the olfactory faculty, the capability to perceive chroma and natural process, and our basic size are characteristics shared by virtually every human inhabitant of the planet. Could we not start with these physical senses rather than with the encultured mind? Could we not make the place pleasurable?

IV.

In historical garden literature a considerable amount of text describes the pleasure of the garden, that is, its comfort, its delight, its sense of well-being. The pleasures of an aristocratic garden in Kyoto backdrop the rather limited action and plot development in the twelfth-century novel, *The Tale of Genji*. Pleasure and its appreciation were so much a part of gardens in the past that we can well wonder why landscape architects today seek significance rather than pleasure. Could it be that pleasure is trite, hedonistic, and ephemeral while meaning is deep and long-lasting? Or perhaps pleasure seems to be too solitary an enterprise while meaning is taken as a collective embodiment of values? Or is it that meaning is the dimension that distinguishes landscape architecture from "mere gardening"?

Roland Barthes argued that to read is to seek the pleasure of the text. He tells us that to provide pleasure "the text must prove to me *that it desires me*" [italics in the original].[47] Knowledge and, a magnificent use of language, plot, and linguistic constructions all contribute to the ultimate goal: the pleasure of reading. Can we not suggest that pleasure is one of the necessary entry points to significance? (Certainly horror would be another, as the sublime school once believed, but our quotidian world seems to provide enough of that.)

It seems curious to me that in most professional design publications the aspect of pleasure is almost completely missing from the discourse, while it thrives in popular gardening magazines and seed catalogs. This is not to say that pursuit of pleasure is not a part of professional work; one assumes that park design, for example, is to a large degree predicated upon the contented use of its grounds. But a discussion of pleasure rarely enters trade and academic landscape writing. Professional publications often talk of the site, the client, the plant materials, perhaps the particular ecological system or cleverness on the designer's part in solving a particularly thorny drainage problem. More recently, some discussion of the alignment of the garden's axis to the summer solstice or its relation to some geomantic construction might also come into play. The lay publications, in contrast, discuss the delight of the garden, and that making one is so easy—like summer cooking recipes—you can do it in, or to, your own back yard. Color and fragrance and delight are givens; and it is the perfect place for a barbecue. Magazines such as *Sunset* have expanded the world of the house and the garden to the world of lifestyle.

Today might be a good time to once more examine the garden in relation to the senses while putting conscious mental rationalizations on the back burner, to create a mixed metaphor. Although the world's peoples vary greatly in terms of linguistic and cultural matrices, we do share roughly similar human senses, although admittedly these can be honed or dimmed by culture. Is there not a link between the senses and significance, or is meaning necessarily restricted to the rational faculties? Barthes would argue that there is a connection. "What is significance?" he writes. "It is meaning, *insofar as it is sensually produced*" [italics in the original].[48]

When an interlocutor once accused Charles Eames of designing furniture only for himself, the designer openly admitted that he did. But he did not design for what was idiosyncratic to himself alone, but what was indicative of the greater population of chair users. Why not re-inject the same sense of pleasing the individual or self into the landscape design? I do not talk here of Gaia and other forms of touchy-feely expression that constitute yet another form of Neo-Archaicism—since telephone lines have superseded lay lines—but of trying to understand at what level our experience can be shared by others. Not as an abstract symbolic system referring back to Celtic times, but places—and ideas—that acknowledge our time, our sensitivities, and our people. This takes more than a pseudo-significant landscape loaded with the designer's explanatory voice-over, or captions built into the landscape itself. It would seem that a designer could create a landscape of pleasure that in itself would become significant. "Art should not simply speak to the mind *through* the senses," wrote Goethe. "[I]t must also satisfy the senses themselves."[49]

There are various arguments for a concern for pleasure in garden design.[50] For one—running the risk of sounding too Californian—pleasure can be a valuable pursuit in itself, as valid as the pursuit of meaning. Even Vitruvius constructed his triad of desirable architectural qualities on commodity, firmness, and delight.[51] In the past, sensory pleasures have served to condition meaning: consider the expression of taste in the selection and arrangement of cut flowers in Japan or the ecstasy of religious experience that underwrote so much Counter-Reformation art and architecture. Sensory experience *moved* the viewer, causing him or her to reflect on religious meaning as well as one's position in the universe—powerful stuff indeed. Third, despite the influence of culture, individual physiological characteristics and even transitory psychological states, pleasure is still more predictable than meaning. As in the past—and despite the collapse of collective social norms—pleasure may provide a more defined path towards meaning than the erudite approaches to landscape design discussed earlier in this paper.

Significance, I believe, is not a designer's construct that benignly accompanies the completion of construction. It is not the product of the maker but is, instead, created by those who follow: those who occupy, confront, and ultimately interpret. Like a patina, significance is acquired only with time. And like a patina, it emerges only if the conditions are right.

ACKNOWLEDGMENTS

I wish to thank Dorothée Imbert, J. B. Jackson, Karen Madsen, Robert Riley, Simon Swaffield, and *Landscape Journal*'s anonymous reader for their perceptive and helpful comments on earlier drafts of this paper. Given the elusive nature of the subject, however, I doubt that I was able to address all their questions and must take responsibility for any shortcomings in both the argument and writing.

NOTES

1 For example, the Fall, 1988, issue of this journal [*Landscape Journal*], guest-edited by Anne Whiston Spirn and called "Nature, Form, and Meaning," was devoted to just this subject. As might be expected, the range of approaches to the subject was broad, and the resulting interpretations broader still.

2 See D. W. Meinig, editor, *The Interpretation of Ordinary Landscapes*, New York: Oxford University Press, 1979. Like anthropologists, cultural geographers read the landscape as a text and are relatively reticent to make judgments about it, much less those of aesthetics. Others, like W. H. Hoskins, however, may decry the modernization of the English landscape and may appraise these residues of cultural process based on personal values. See W. H. Hoskins, *The Making of the English Landscape*, Harmondsworth: Penguin Books, 1955, and compare with J. B. Jackson, *Landscapes*, Amherst, MA: University of Massachusetts Press, 1970.

3 Mark Francis and Randolph T. Hester, Jr., editors, *The Meaning of Gardens*, Cambridge, MA: MIT Press, 1989. The book, developed from a conference held at the University of California at Davis in 1987, should be distinguished from the previously released typescript and un-illustrated proceedings.

4 Robert B. Riley, "From Sacred Grove to Disney World: The Search for Garden Meaning," *Landscape Journal*, Number 2, Fall, 1988, p. 138. Whether Riley's statement encompasses history as well as contemporary life was not spelled out. The author's hesitation to assign meaning to gardens may stem from the pluralistic and multi-cultural composition of today's American population. One could add, somewhat desperately perhaps, that this admittedly diverse population appears to be bent on expressing its constitution of differing cultural groups rather than examining the shared characteristics of all human beings.

5 Laurie Olin, "Form, Meaning, and Expression in Landscape Architecture," *Landscape Journal*, Number 2, Fall,

1988, p. 159. The problems that develop from dividing the production of meaning into distinct categories are obvious to the author of the article as well as to its readers. I imagine that Olin would agree that meaning ultimately derives from both categories operating simultaneously.

6 Olin's classifications roughly parallel the two categories I had once proposed in discussing the idea of formalism in the landscape. The first, *trace*, was the unintentioned marking or making of space through use. The second, *intent*, concerned conscious spatial definition and/or construction that considered dimensions beyond that of function; that is, the semantic as well as the syntactic aspects of landscape design. Marc Treib, "Traces upon the Land: The Formalistic Landscape," *Architectural Association Quarterly*, Volume 1, Number 4, 1979. Reprinted in Marc Treib, *Settings and Stray Paths: Writings on Landscapes and Gardens*, London: Routledge, 2003.

7 The library on meaning in philosophy is vast and makes trying reading. The award for the most provocative title should probably be given to the Cambridge dons C. K. Ogden and I. A. Richards, *The Meaning of Meaning*, New York: Harcourt, Brace & World, Inc., 1923. If one accepted their definition of meaning in *language*

and extended it to *landscape architecture*, one would have to agree that it was indeed possible to design meaning into landscapes: "The meaning of any sentence is what the speaker intends to be understood from it by the listener" (p. 193). The authors, obviously, make no such claim for landscape design, however, nor do they imply that linguistic theory is applicable in any form to the making of landscape.

8 For example, I am told that—like landscape meaning—there remains no clear definition of electricity. This has not hampered our ability to understand, produce, modulate, and utilize the resource, however. Louis Armstrong is said to have said that if he had to explain jazz to someone, they would never really understand it. This just may be true of meaning as well.

9 That this stance is problematic seems obvious.

10 Tunnard's essays that would constitute his 1938 *Gardens in the Modern Landscape* appeared serially in *Architectural Review* starting the previous year. About the same time, James Rose contributed a series of articles to *Pencil Points*, the predecessor of today's *Progressive Architecture*, including one essay entitled "Plants Dictate Garden Form" written in 1938. The conclusions that Rose reached in this essay closely paralleled

those of Tunnard. Both included a list of plant materials suitable for modern conditions.

11 Conversation with the author, June, 1988.

12 The notable exception was the work of Roberto Burle Marx, who would frequently be characterized as a "painter in plants" who drew on the shapes of modern, often non-objective, art. See Marc Treib, "Axioms for a Modern Landscape Architecture," in Marc Treib, editor, *Modern Landscape Architecture: A Critical Review*, Cambridge, MA: MIT Press, 1993.

In a series of articles published in *Architectural Record* at the beginning of the 1940s Rose, Eckbo, and Dan Kiley linked the physical and social environment from the intimate to regional scales as a prerequisite of responsible landscape architecture. They did not talk of significance, however, but implied that meaning accompanies an intelligent design, or that it was just not an issue. These articles have been republished in Treib, *Modern Landscape Architecture*, cited above.

13 In Gideon's eyes, space was the primary quest of modern architecture, the realization of an adventure he traced back to Baroque spatial planning in Rome under Sixtus V and the undulating facades of Francesco Borromini. Sigfried Gideon, *Space, Time and Architecture*, Cambridge, MA: Harvard University Press, 1938. The quest reached an apogee in Bruno Zevi's *Architecture as Space*, New York: Horizon Press, 1957.

14 For a representative collection of Greenberg's ideas and writings, see Clement Greenberg, *Art and Culture: Critical Essays*, Boston: Beacon Press, 1961.

15 Garrett Eckbo, *Landscapes for Living*, New York: Reinhold Publishing, 1950. See also Reuben Rainey, "'Organic Form in the Humanized Landscape': Garrett Eckbo's *Landscapes for Living*," in Treib, *Modern Landscape Architecture*, pp. 180–205.

16 Ian McHarg, *Design with Nature*, Garden City, NY: Doubleday, 1969. Despite his predominant polemic and pervasive rationale, McHarg admits moments of poetry and suggestions of meaning: "The best symbol of peace might better be the garden than the dove" (p. 5).

17 Olin, "Form, Meaning, and Expression," pp. 150–151.

18 To my mind, one of the real burdens of landscape architecture is that two professions are combined under the same name, as if their interests and goals were coincident. Landscape architecture is concerned with forming, as well as planning, a landscape;

landscape management or planning, with its regulation. Obviously, they overlap in their concern with living systems, but landscape architecture requires active formal intervention in a way that regional planning does not. This is not to say, however, that they both do not have consequences in the form of the landscape.

19 In his 1984 *California Scenario* plaza/garden in Costa Mesa, California, Noguchi appears to have adapted a wedge-shaped fragment of the astronomical observatory for use as a water source. While this element can also be read as a modernist abstraction of a hill, the form bears a striking resemblance to its Indian predecessor. Noguchi's program for the garden encompassed the various ecological zones of California, from mountain meadow to desert: an attempt at evoking the genius loci and creating meaning?

20 Gary Dwyer, "The Power under Our Feet," *Landscape Architecture*, May–June, 1986, pp. 65–68. The choice of Ogham as the script with which to inscribe the fault line was based on its formal properties alone: it is written as cross marks across a linear spine. Dwyer himself asks the critical question: "How can an ancient Celtic language have anything to do with the San Andreas Fault?" And

replies: "Aside from its development by a primitive people who were rhythmically allied with the forces of nature, Ogham began like all languages with the mark, with 'naming the unknowable.'" The substantiation remains unconvincing.

21 After an exhaustive search, and a telephone call to the author, I have been unable to find the exact source of the quotation, or even whether this was the exact quotation. If not precisely those words, the spirit of Professor Howett's observation is captured by them.

22 Christian Norberg-Schulz determined three ways in which man-made places relate to nature. The first regards rendering the natural structure "more precise"; in the second, construction complements the natural order, while the third symbolizes it: "The purpose of symbolization is to free the meaning from the immediate situation, whereby it becomes a 'cultural object,' which may form part of a more complex situation, or be moved to another place," *Genius Loci*, New York: Rizzoli, 1980, p. 17. Edward Relph's *Place and Placelessness* constitutes, in some ways, the complement to Norberg-Schulz's more natural-oriented vision. Relph also includes the symbolic as part of the triad of factors that create the sense of place: "The identity of a place is

comprised of three interrelated components, each irreducible to the other —physical features or appearance, observable activities and functions, and meanings or symbols." London: Pion Limited, 1976, p. 61.

23 My anecdote is a paraphrase of a citizen reaction I overheard in 1990 when photographing an urban triangle in Washington, D.C., planted by Oehme/ Van Sweden. My kibitzer read my taking of photographs as documenting a deplorable urban condition, presumably as evidence to have the wrong righted as soon as possible. This was in spite of the fact that numerous plaques identified the various grasses, a clueing at a second level that the wild look was intentional.

24 I realize, of course, that there are far more considerations bearing on these decisions than the aesthetic alone. But at some point in the process, aesthetic questions must be addressed.

25 "If one wishes to work on the cutting edge in either fine art or design," writes Martha Schwartz, "one must be informed of developments in the world of painting and sculpture. Ideas surface more quickly in painting and sculpture than in architecture or landscape architecture, due to many factors including the immediacy of the media and the relative low investment of money required to explore an idea." "Landscape and Common Culture," in Treib, *Modern Landscape Architecture*, p. 264. As is often the case, however, by the time art ideas are applied to landscape design, they are a bit tired and worn. For a passionate argument for the Neo-Archaic in art—one source of landscape architecture in the 1980s— see Lucy Lippard, *Overlays*, New York: E. P. Dutton, 1983.

26 Norma Evenson, *Paris: A Century of Change*, New Haven, CT: Yale University Press, 1978. Or taken at rush hours, as a round and linear parking lot. In fact, one of the slaughter houses at La Villette, la Halle aux Boeufs, was renovated into an art space by Reichen and Robert in 1985; a modern recent structure for animal dispatch was heroically recast as the City of Science and Industry by Adrian Fainsilber in 1987 and is the park's principal attraction.

27 The notable exception is Alexandre Chemetoff's *Sequence IV* or Bamboo Garden. Given its sense of path, its enclosure, and its Didactic revelation of subterranean services, the bamboo garden is both a lesson and respite from both the city and the other parts of the park at La Villette. As of June, 1993, however, it had become overgrown and is in need of pruning and reformation.

28 Much of what has been written perpetuates the designer's original claims; many of the authors seem never to have visited the actual park and their writings are discourse about discourse.

29 According to J. B. Jackson, expediency is a hallmark of vernacular building. *Defining the Vernacular Landscape*, New Haven, CT: Yale University Press, 1984.

30 This friend, who happens to be French and writes about modernist French gardens, wishes to remain anonymous.

31 Added in 2003: Since this essay first appeared, the movement has gained greater visibility under the name "eco-revelatory design." See *Landscape Journal*, "Eco-Revelatory Design: Nature Constructued/Nature Revealed," 1998.

32 Garreau offers two "laws" that govern the naming of developments. First, there is Jake Page's Law of Severed Continuity: "You name a place for what is no longer there as a result of your actions." Next, "The Keith Severin Corollary": "All subdivisions are named after whatever species are first driven out by the construction. E.g.: Quail Trail Estates." In "The Laws: How We Live," *Edge City*, Garden City, NY: Doubleday, 1991, pp. 461–471.

33 Sir Geoffrey Jellicoe's proposal for the Moody Gardens in Galveston was essentially a landscape theme park, evoking (but not copying) historical garden types. Jellicoe, *Landscapes of Civilization*, Woodbridge, UK: Garden Art Press, 1989.

34 There is some indication that they do. Particularly in good weather, the less formal areas of the "gardens in movement" are highly utilized, perhaps because they provide some of the only truly private—and shaded —spaces in what is otherwise a highly structured ensemble. In that way, they resemble the country in comparison to the city.

Added in 2010: *More than fifteen years have passed since the* Jardin en mouvement *was planted, and over the years the variety of species has declined as the shrubs have matured.*

35 I realize that there is quite another school of thought that regards both human experience and significance as more or less universal. This belief has produced "pattern languages," among other theories, derived from a selective potpourri of peoples and places, with the assumption that the proper blend (selected and structured by the authors) will perfectly suit all of humanity—certainly, at least twentieth-century America. My own experience through travel and reading—supported

by historical study—suggests quite the opposite; that is, that values are not universal, but instead particular to a people, place, and time. Perhaps this could be appropriately termed "cultural relativism"—and it probably has been so termed by someone somewhere.

36 Thus, Japanese gardens built outside Japan are mere shadows of their referents, since they lack their native cultural matrix. They become "japanesque" and expose physical features as a photograph captures an image but only rarely the essence of subject.

37 Polite, like the term Monumental or High Style, is used in this essay in (near) opposition to the Vernacular tradition of landscape making and building. It implies neither a rank ordering of one above the other nor any particular character—except that the Polite tradition will normally approach environmental design far more self-consciously than the Vernacular.

38 "It is doubtless a difficult notion to appreciate today, but in the eighteenth century all the fine arts were deemed to have representation at their center, and gardening aspired to *beaux-arts* status," John Dixon Hunt, "The Garden as Cultural Object," in Howard Adams and Stewart Wrede, editors, *Denatured Visions*, New York: Museum of Modern Art, 1991, p. 26.

39 Ibid., p. 28.

40 Ibid.

41 In his or her notes, the reader anonymously reviewing a draft of this essay for *Landscape Journal* wisely noted two categories of meaning: "A. Systems of Signification/ Representation in the landscape (metaphysical, narrative, allegorical, symbolic), and B. Circumstances of engagement with the landscape (experiential, sensory, physical)." This might be interpreted broadly as a meaning that accrues perceptually as opposed to meaning that accrues conceptually.

42 It would be interesting to return to the Vietnam Memorial in a hundred years' time to determine whether the design and the inscribed names would retain their effect.

43 Folk cultures have been described as those which are geographically delimited, developing only slowly over time. Mass culture, in contrast, is more broadly ranged and changes rapidly.

44 Or as Robert Riley put it: "Such a lack of shared symbolism does not rule out the garden as a carrier of powerful meaning but it does discount the likelihood of meanings that speak strongly to the whole society." Riley, "From Sacred Grove to Disney World," p. 142.

45 J. B. Jackson, among others, has pointed out that the ocularcentric garden is a Renaissance development and that during the medieval and earlier ages the correspondences between plant and cosmos were firmly established. The form of the plant or its fragrance or its name suggested its value through associations. A yellow plant might be appropriate for curing jaundice; a round one might assuage headaches. Those that cared about such things—admittedly, a small community—were bound together in a common belief system through Christianity. "Gardens to Decipher and Garden to Admire," in *The Necessity for Ruins*, Amherst, MA: University of Massachusetts Press, 1980, pp. 37–54.

46 Robert Riley cited Mary Douglas's term "condensed symbols" that "carry not just one meaning but accretions of many meanings, layered upon each other and over time. They are symbols that are commonly agreed upon, not designer-chosen, that connote deep affective meaning, not quick cleverness, and that are integral to a context that is culturally agreed upon as appropriate." Riley, "From Sacred Grove to Disney World," p. 142.

47 "Does our involvement for publication enter here? While neither meaning nor pleasure can be photographed, there can be pleasure depicted within a photograph; the photograph itself can provide pleasure, of course." Roland Barthes, *The Pleasure of the Text*, New York: Hill and Wang, 1975, p. 6.

48 Ibid.

49 J. W. von Goethe, "The Collector and His Circle," *Propyläen* **II**, 1799, in John Gage, *Goethe on Art*, Berkeley: University of California Press, 1980, p. 70.

50 My own thoughts on this subject have been greatly augmented by suggestions from Robert Riley, for which I am grateful.

51 Vitruvius, of course, spoke Latin, not English. This particular rendering of the Latin original is by Henry Wotten.

Commentary 2:

Must Landscapes Mean?

Revisited

Marc Treib

My own interest in meaning, I suspect, derived from my involvement with architectural theory and history. When I entered the teaching arena in the late 1960s, architecture was energetically—I might say desperately—searching for models for its theory. This interest in theory in all the design professions probably stemmed from pressures from the university to become more academic, to provide an education rather than a training, to be more a discipline than a profession. We didn't question these pressures, unfortunately, and they continue today with the sciences being used more and more to provide models for, and evaluate, the humanities. As noted in the introduction to this book, architecture sought a model for theory from a broad and continually changing series of fields.

When I drifted into the arena of landscape architecture I found little evidence of parallel searches for theory. (It came some years later.) Now, I'm still not sure what theory is in the design professions —certainly it varies markedly from theory in the sciences. But let us accept that it involves standards and values by which we generate

126 /

our working methods and forms, and evaluate their viability. What, or whom, I did encounter was Ian McHarg and *Design with Nature*. The advent of ecology saved landscape architecture, at least at Berkeley where the department was seriously threatened by closure, given its purported concern for only making gardens. But McHarg— and one would need to add Rachel Carson—offered theory (I'll use that troublesome word) from within the discipline rather than borrowed from without. But there was a chronic problem in this fixation on ecology (now returning to us in discussions of sustainability, by the way): How did *people* fit into this analysis and planning, and for that matter what about landscape architecture as a cultural and social practice? At this point in time I believe we are well aware of the limits of McHargian thinking—Susan Herrington and Anne Whiston Spirn, among others, have cautioned us on this point.

So that is the background for my interest in meaning. Background only. But what really prompted me to write the piece "Must Landscapes Mean?" were the piles—or was it reams?—of hyperbole and extravagant claims that accompanied the presentations of their design schemes by practitioners and especially by students. Why should I be convinced that a design is valid because the pattern of its paths traced the lines of railroad tracks that once crossed the site—long gone, long buried, today covered by second-growth woods? Why should I think a landscape is nifty because it used chain-link fence painted in lurid pink, or for that matter, because it made a virtue of rainwater in stormy times—although it looked like an untended vacant lot in the dry months that prevailed? Why should an alignment with the solar solstice make a crappy design laudable? These weighed on my fragile mind and the only way to get rid of them was to write something, hopefully for *Landscape Journal*. After the reviewers got through with their work on the first version of my text it was obvious I would need to clarify my thoughts and bolster the background for my observations. Robert Riley, then editor, suggested I look at Laurie Olin's "Form, Meaning, and Expression in Landscape

Architecture," published in 1988—which in some ways was the origin of the panel at the 2009 annual meeting of the Council of Educators in Landscape Architecture and, ultimately, of this book.

The opening of my own text traced much of the same ground I have just spoken about, making reference in appropriate places to philosophers like Nelson Goodman, as well as C. K. Ogden and I. A. Richards, the title of whose book *The Meaning of Meaning* I have perennially envied. I wondered why this discussion of meaning in landscape architecture had started in the 1980s. Was there a neat, if belated, parallel with colleagues in art and architecture and literary criticism? In the middle section of the paper, I suggested that there were six ways, taken alone or in groups, that designers discussed meaning in relation to their work:

1. Neo-Archaic refers to the constructions of preliterate cultures, places like Stonehenge and burial mounds like Kivic in Sweden. These first influenced the work of the land artists, Robert Smithson for example—his 1970 *Spiral Hill* in Emmen, Holland, today a bit overgrown—and the spiral hill that appeared in a Hargreaves Associates project in Denver. Presumably, if there was meaning once, deep down in our history and heritage, we can excavate it, use it, and it will be equally relevant today. Alas, it's not that easy.

2. Although the Latin term *genius loci* dates from ancient times, we know it as the Genius of the Place from Alexander Pope's "Epistle to Lord Burlington," in which he instructs m'lord to reject formalities such as allées and topiary. Instead, he should look more carefully at the site and use what it offers as the basis for improvement. Ah, this is a wonderful direction in the eighteenth-century agricultural, Georgic landscape of England but far more problematic today in American suburbia or the wastelands of brownfield sites. More difficult, but no less valid, of course.

3. Zeitgeist is the German term, much used in art and architectural circles, for "the spirit of the times." In art this led to impressionism, cubism, surrealism, and a lot of other isms. In landscape design this

led to looking at art, and to a lesser degree architecture, as a source of vocabulary—one wanted to be contemporary, of course. Garrett Eckbo used the paintings of Wassily Kandinsky as the basis for some of his designs, the work of the architect Ludwig Mies van der Rohe —especially his 1929 German Pavilion in Barcelona—for others. Bernard Tschumi looked to Russian Constructivism when he designed the Parc de la Villette, in particular the architectural fantasies of Iakov Chernikov.

4. The distinction between High and Low cultures remains problematic, tied in with the nasty aspects of elitism and paternalism. But if we adopt the materials and look of vernacular culture, do we not bridge the gap that normally exists between them? Not. When Martha Schwartz takes the solitary mirror ball from the vernacular backyard and uses it in multiples, in lines—paired with alignments of trees and stone paths—the meaning is hardly the same. We could term this appropriation rather than bridging, however good the original intention.

5. Didactic landscapes supposedly accrue their meaning by instructing those who experience them into the processes, if not always wonders, of nature. Most commonly these days, the subject is stormwater management, but native species or plant restoration are other popular subjects. By making reference to processes that take place on site, they de facto refer to the genius of the place, and like several of these categories, they may be applied in pairs.

6. Themed landscapes, normally gardens, "celebrate" (and that's the word that's most often used) one aspect of nature's panoply. This nothing new. Vita Sackville-West and Harold Nicholson created a White Garden at Sissinghurst. Fredrik Magnus Piper made Turkish pavilions and copper tents at Drottningholm and Haga in Sweden. These are pleasant themes. Less pleasant was Gunther Vogt's *Garden of Violence* at the Swiss Expo in 2002—but how violent it actually was is open to question—as is the very idea of injecting meaning into natural forms normally encountered in rather benign circumstances.

Seen today, the neo-archaic has more or less disappeared as have references to vernacular landscapes, except in the greater context of cultural landscape. Zeitgeist has been superseded by concerns for sustainability; themes, I suppose, will always be around whether as cancer survivors' gardens or the biblical plant areas of botanical gardens. The didactic urge still reigns: for example, in revealing natural processes as a means of educating the public—tied, again, to sustainability.

Ultimately, I would suspect that the most enduring element of the original essay is not these categories but my assertion—which I still believe—that in today's America, with its fractious and multi-cultural composition, meaning is constructed over time through a transaction between people and place—and that ultimately it is personal. In a folk society where values, beliefs, signs, and symbols are all shared, where each member is essentially indoctrinated into these systems from birth until death, imbuing meaning is possible. But those times and conditions are long gone in contemporary society. Jane Gillette argued persuasively against the inherent meaning in gardens, to some degree reinforcing my point that we the users make meaning, that it is not latent in the place itself—no matter what the designer would like to believe. On the other hand, this provides an excellent argument for rendering the maker and the user congruent, that is, for participation in the design process. Meaning, however, is hardly the same as aesthetic satisfaction.

The Swiss philologist Ferdinand de Saussure, writing early in the twentieth century, proposed the terms *langue* (language), and *parole* (speech), as rudiments of human communication [figures 2-11A, 2-11B]. Language covers the grammar and words, the structure and the material. Speech is the work of the individual. It allows every member of a linguistic family to create sentences that no one has ever heard before—and yet that sentence is intelligible. What that sentence means, however, is ultimately personal.

2-11A

DIAGRAM ILLUSTRATING THE *LANGUE / PAROLE* RELATIONSHIP.

2-11B

DIAGRAM ILLUSTRATING THE CULTURE / MEANING RELATIONSHIP.

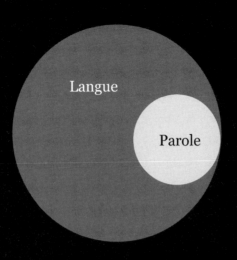

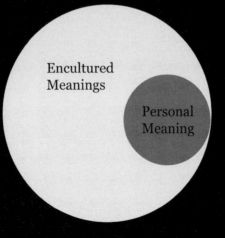

Meaning in built form—I include art and landscape design in this category—follows such a pattern. We are formed and circumscribed by our culture and our times, but we make interpretations based on our own experience and knowledge. If not, we have been indoctrinated to a degree that is best termed repressive. Meaning is fluid and changes with time as well as the individual: even meanings that are lucid today become obscure in the future as society and its symbolic systems evolve.

I ended "Must Landscapes Mean?" with the observation that although we may never agree on meaning, we might accept common conditions for pleasure. We are roughly the same size and weight—well, within a given range—although various peoples have adjusted to specific climatic conditions. Why is the discussion of pleasure missing from our professional journals—especially those that are refereed? In contrast, pleasure often prevails as a subject of interest in popular shelter and garden magazines. So let me leave it at that —meaning and pleasure. The two are not mutually exclusive. In fact, great pleasure can lead to some very significant landscape meanings—especially in gardens, in the woods, perhaps at the beach, or under the grandstands at a high school football game.

2-12
NORAH LINDSAY,
THE LONG GARDEN,
CLIVEDEN, ENGLAND,
c. 1900.
[MARC TREIB]

3.

Can Gardens Mean?

Jane Gillette   [2005]

In a perceptive article that questions the pursuit of meaning in landscape architecture projects of the 1980s and 1990s, Marc Treib asks, "Must Landscapes Mean?"[1] What happens if, instead of asking "Must Landscapes Mean?" we ask "Can Gardens Mean?" I consider the possibility that real gardens are by definition incapable of meaning anything, or anything much, and that the strength of the garden— its ability to provide beauty and delight—lies in this very incapacity. In this essay, I will strengthen the less frequently defended side of what is admittedly an old debate, one that nevertheless still remains current in landscape architecture discourse. My argument, generated as part of a study of meaning in fictional gardens, contains an important, if unstated, subtext: that real gardens are different from gardens in novels, which must mean because they have no other function. I contend that it is very difficult for the garden designer to express complex ideas using

3-1

ANDROPOGON ASSOCIATES,
AVALON PARK,
STONY BROOK HARBOR,
NEW YORK, 2001.
[CAROL FRANKLIN]

only garden elements, and certainly very difficult for an audience to "read" the results. When I talk about the construction of meaning, I am not thinking about the intervention of the human mind (which of course is involved in the design of gardens) but, rather, about the use of discursive reasoning, primarily language. Hence, if I go to what may seem ridiculous lengths to prove the case against meaning, it is in order to consider, in due course, how the relatively mute condition of the real garden makes it such fertile ground for the novelist.[2]

GARDEN ORIGINS AND THE PATHETIC FALLACY

My contention that the denial of meaning is an integral feature of the garden may at first seem startling. Actually, it is a notion more generally accepted than stated, one that can be detected in a range of evidence. Indeed, the deceptive essence of the garden may well lie in its origins. Imagine, for a moment, the planting of the first garden, an unverifiable event. It was undoubtedly a small gesture, but one that occurred after humans had begun to plant food crops. That advance was conceivably initiated by some keen observer who saw an edible plant growing accidentally on a garbage heap or in an area used as a privy. Deciding to perform an experiment, the original farmer took a seed and stuck it down into whatever waste material was at hand. It grew into an edible plant and the agricultural revolution was under way. We can also imagine that having asserted their power against the environment and finding that they could control the vegetable aspect of what we conveniently call nature, these new agriculturists felt a great loss and a greater dread—like toddlers who take their first steps and immediately begin to suffer the anxieties of parental separation. Human beings had acquired power but only at the cost of consciously experiencing themselves as set apart from the rest of the physical universe, from nature, which thus became the material on which human consciousness works its will.[3]

Let us now imagine that to alleviate those anxieties, in a process similar to the drawing of edible deerlike creatures on the walls of caves, some imaginative soul resurrected the old unbroken association with the vegetable world by growing a few plants—plants not intended for food but simply for the enjoyment of smelling, watching, touching, and nurturing—in short, a garden where human beings could involve themselves with the vegetable world. Although this account of the origin of the garden is admittedly speculative, it would accord with a feature so constant that John Dixon Hunt, among others, has made it part of his definition of the garden: the inclusion within the garden's boundaries of references to agriculture. Presumably the garden (Third Nature) could not have come into existence without some prior consideration of wilderness (First Nature) and agriculture (Second Nature). In *Greater Perfections: The Practice of Garden Theory*, Hunt defines the garden as a bounded space that makes reference to the world beyond its boundaries, but his definition is far from prescriptive: "What is necessary here is only to insist that the third nature of gardens is best considered as existing in terms of the other two."[4]

Hunt attributes this outside referencing to the garden maker's desire to epitomize the whole world within the limited spaces of the garden, in other words, to recapture all of nature within the garden. But how does human consciousness fit into such inclusive schemes? I suggest the following proposition: that First Nature was experienced by the undivided, unconscious self; that Second Nature established a separation between the self and what we call nature; and that Third Nature attempts to reconstitute the old unity. One popular banality is that the gardener is on his knees praying to God. It seems more likely that he is on his knees searching for his old undivided, unselfconscious self.

Evidence to support this proposition exists in the thousands upon thousands of practical books on gardening. Consider their subject matter. Most detail the information needed by the gardener to keep plants alive and thriving. Next to the necessity for unrelenting work, such information is the theme of garden books—and one that leads almost inevitably to a version of the pathetic fallacy (the attribution of human traits to inanimate nature). Of the thousands of possible choices, listen to the voice of Margery Fish, a popular English garden writer from the 1950s and 1960s, in the following passages. She describes some "*H. orientalis*, which thrives in the cold…I can see them from my desk bravely standing up to the worst weather of the winter and I admire their fortitude and grace." She characterizes *S. argentea* as "one of the handsomest of the silver tribe" but cautions that "it does not care for too much rain on its thick felted leaves and is happier if you can find a corner for it where it can grow vertically, which is not too easy with such a big person."[5] Of *Physostegia* Vivid, she writes, "Like many other plants that increase underground it flowers best in rather a constricted area, like a narrow bed beside a path, where it has no temptation to stray and waste its substance on underground roots instead of lovely orchid-coloured flowers."[6] And *P. heterophyllus* True Blue, Fish tells us, "does not care much for lime, and behaves best in an acid soil. I give her plenty of peat and she responds like a lady."[7]

Of course I quote Fish because her work provides an extreme example. Yet she is like many less accomplished garden writers in succumbing to the pathetic fallacy so consistently that after a while it hardly seems fallacious to attribute likes and dislikes, longings and repugnancies to creatures who, while inanimate in the sense of lacking consciousness, nevertheless do live and die by needs strongly resembling choices—or so those needs must seem to the emotionally involved gardeners who desire only to keep their plants alive and flourishing.

My speculative origin of the garden tries, then, to account for a salient feature of all gardens, from a row of flowers along a fence in Grandmother's backyard to Henry Hoare's Stourhead. This salient feature is the one essential function of the garden: to give pleasure of a certain mindless sort. If it is true that much of the pleasure we derive from the garden depends on denying the separation between conscious man and the rest of nature, then the development of the garden may be considered the elaboration of a complex lie. Alternatively, as we learn more about animal behavior, the genetic code, and the mysterious relationship of matter and consciousness, the garden may turn out to be the long-term articulation of a truth. But for the thousand or so years covered by garden history, it seems possible to say that, by and large, the garden has flourished by denying the close investigation of a whole realm of ideas.

And what are these ideas? We can find them assembled most compactly in Clarence Glacken, *Traces on the Rhodian Shore: Nature and Culture in Western Thought from Ancient Times to the End of the Eighteenth Century.*[8] In Glacken's masterpiece of intellectual history we learn about the scores of Western philosophers who thoroughly addressed the nature/culture relationship, one that they usually stated in terms of separation and frequently in terms of opposition. Some philosophers posited a parallel between humans and nature—for example, in the physiology of the humours—but most depicted an abrupt disjuncture between man and nature. Humanity affects nature, nature affects humanity, but usually the philosophers could explain what they frequently characterized as the wondrous perfection of nature by positing the existence of a transcendent god, a Great Designer whose work can only be appreciated by a humankind created in his own image and so privileged above the rest of creation.

GARDEN MEANING IN POSTMODERN CULTURE

I realize that to equate meaning with the works of Glacken's philosophers sets a rather high standard for meaning. I must also admit I sympathize with Treib, who nicely points out in "Must Landscapes Mean?" that his "own effort will probably be no different from that of almost all previous writers" because he "will discuss the question of significance without precisely defining it." He does, nevertheless, try. "We can," Treib writes, "at least establish a broad theater in which meaning is taken simply as an integral aspect of human lives, beyond any basic attachment to the land through familiarity. Meaning thus comprises ethics, values, history, affect, all of them taken singly or as a group." Although valiant, Treib's definition seems unmanageably broad. By this definition, what would not constitute meaning? More important, his definition suggests no subject, no area of significance, that could only be expressed by the garden. Behind this observation lies my critical assumption that every medium champions itself; so that if people make gardens to express ideas, we need to ask what idea requires the garden for its full and best expression, an expression that cannot be adequately achieved by some other medium—poetry, say, or the philosophical treatise, the play, the landscape painting.

Even though Treib does not go so far as to say that meaning requires words, he does point out the prevalence of written and spoken explanations in the promotion of consciously designed meaningful landscapes. He notes "the declarations of meaning" that in the 1980s "began to accompany the published photographs and drawings of landscape designs"; the presence at conferences of landscape architects who "would describe their intentions, their sources, and what the designs meant"; the existence in many a designed landscape of a plaque— "plastic or metal"—that "provides its meaning to the residents with credits to the designer, the sponsoring body, and of course the mayor in office at the time." And he points out how frequently statements are needed to alert us to the meaning of these designs, in one case (Parc de la Villette) acknowledging that "what has been written about the project is far more intriguing than what one encounters on site."[9] According to Treib the expression of meaning became so important to landscape designers in the 1980s and 1990s because they were reacting to the anti-historical bias of the Modernist movement. Although this reason alone seems insufficient it does point to a certain time frame that includes a number of other developments.

1. We are living in a period in which design crafts of all sorts have been ratcheted up to the level of art by the assumption of a useful formula: Craft + Meaning = Art. This period has also been distinguished by a vehement anti-capitalist, anti-consumer rhetoric—which, ironically, keeps step with the insistent beat of consumerism. This rhetoric tends to elevate changes in style by attributing them to something more noble than mere usefulness in marketing. The implied suggestion is, frequently, that they are due to a change in meaning.

2. The main reason for increased concern with meaning probably lies in the popularity of modern and postmodern ideas—first in philosophy, then in art and literary criticism, much later in architectural criticism, and finally in landscape architectural criticism. Landscape architects vehemently dislike architectural priority, but it seems fair to wonder if landscape architecture academics would have become so determined to find meaning in landscape design had not architecture academics led the way by finding so much meaning in architecture.

3. Our concern with meaning may also have intensified because, for the last two hundred years or so, criticism of all sorts has moved from a concern with the intention of the artist to the creation of meaning by the audience. In so doing criticism has, not surprisingly, privileged the theorist and the critic—who always use words to articulate meaning—over such creators as novelists, poets, painters, and

so forth, who generally have other arrows in their quivers besides logical, discursive, articulated meaning.[10]

These overlapping occurrences lead to an uneasy thought: Has embarrassment driven designers into an exaggerated concern with the expression of meaning in their gardens? If meaning is out there all about us, easily discovered in absolutely every human artifact, how can the garden designer simply admit to doing nothing beyond composing beautiful places in a continuing succession of styles meant to please the users of the place? Would designers living in an elevated cultural atmosphere want to admit to such superficiality? Some landscape architects may think that to create beautiful and functional places is more than sufficient, but how hard it is to resist stepping into the arena with practitioners from other fields—postmodern literary critics, for example, or movie directors, who are our most revered artists.

PROBLEMS OF LANGUAGE AND REPRESENTATION

And yet can the garden designer generate complex significance? Let us consider an obvious fact: Gardens have physical form and actuality, they are made up of real things that take up space, and since they are composed of natural materials and generally located out-of-doors, they are subject to natural laws—of weather, seasonal change, growth and decay, gravity, entropy, and so forth. The essential difficulty that designers face when they decide to make a landscape mean is the material quality of the tools they have at hand. These include a host of elements: water in the form of lakes, rivers, and fountains; paving of all sorts; walls, benches, paths, and statuary; grading; follies that range from grottos to temples; and flowers, trees, stones, and shrubs. These elements, which the designer has at his or her disposal, may be called vocabulary, and the way the designer combines them may be called syntax. This is, however, a metaphorical usage in which material elements and the way they are combined are said to be like vocabulary and syntax in written and spoken language. Actually, they are very different: the material sort of vocabulary and syntax lacks the flexibility and range of vocabulary and syntax in language.

Perhaps the most serious problem that confronts designers who seek to express meaning in the garden is representation. Part of the pleasure of experiencing art lies in distinguishing between what is being said and how it is being said. Indeed, the distinction is probably necessary. When something and the representation of that something coincide, we are left uncertain as to what meaning, if any at all, the creator intends. In experiencing physical landscapes, it is frequently difficult to distinguish between the artifact and the meaning of the artifact, between the container of meaning and the contents.[11]

To clarify this point, let us consider a garden type that seems to have more meaning than most: the fifteenth-century Japanese dry garden, which expresses the unity of all phenomena, spiritual and material, human and nonhuman. This is, conceivably, the only meaning of all gardens, but this garden articulates it—that is, draws the unconscious meaning up into consciousness. We notice that the expressive strength of this sort of garden lies in a clear demarcation of the container, a convention borrowed from Northern Song landscape painting. We must view the garden from the temple, for it stands apart and is not to be entered. Furthermore we frequently see the garden backed by a blank wall. This wall provides the equivalent of the background of a painting or a sample of calligraphy so that the elements in the garden can seem like brush strokes on silk. Such devices alert us to the fact that we are seeing a work of art, one that represents an idea. By contrast, how many of us have walked through a perfectly beautiful landscape by Andropogon and never suspected that something meaningful was afoot [figure 3-1]? This unconsciousness is part of Andropogon's design intent.

143 /

It is necessary to point out, nevertheless, that in addition to its framing devices, the meaning of the dry garden is established by a written and spoken tradition. If we were to come upon a dry garden separate from its temple setting, if we were ignorant of Buddhism, we would not be able to tell from the garden alone what it means. Indeed, the dry garden depends on our recognizing in a feeling manner the truth of its meaning, and millions of tourists have conceivably confronted the dry garden without really understanding what it expresses. It could also be said that once we recognize what a dry garden means we perceive that it is selling water by the river for we can begin to recognize the meaning of the garden everywhere, both within the garden and without.

What is called vocabulary in landscape design is particularly susceptible to the problem of representation. Anne Whiston Spirn praises the superiority of what she calls the language of landscape:

Verbal and mathematical languages, the word and the formula, merely describe and interpret the world for they are not the things they describe, but always one or more steps removed. In landscape, representation and reality fuse when a tree, path, or gate is invested with larger significance. In a sacred landscape, a path is seldom only a path, but the Path, where pilgrims climb to reach a hilltop shrine tracing a metaphorical and an actual journey.[12]

It is, however, this very lack of fusion that makes verbal language such a useful tool for conveying meaning. A word or a formula is never the same thing as what it represents, so it cannot be mistaken for it. It always describes or represents something else. When we see the words "path" and "Path," we cannot make the mistake of believing that they refer to exactly the same thing. The word "path" refers to a functional means of getting from one place to another; the word "Path" refers to a path that someone has imbued with a special significance (perhaps its universality) signaled by that capital letter. A writer/speaker can use a word "path" to refer to something slightly different from a path (an animal track, say) or something entirely different (a spiritual quest). Such is the nature of metaphor in linguistic constructions. A path is like a spiritual quest. A path is also profoundly not at all like a quest. If the "like" is articulated, the device is called a simile; if it is omitted, it is a metaphor. The writer can make the connection clearer by capitalizing the P. Looking at an actual path in the landscape, we cannot tell if, in addition to being the way we get somewhere else, it has been meaningfully distinguished as a spiritual element in a sacred landscape—unless we already know or are told by some other means (like a sign). For example, we know from outside knowledge that the path from the gate to the door of a traditional Japanese teahouse has a spiritual dimension, but we cannot know that simply by looking at it. In and of itself, it cannot convey this meaning.

Consider another limitation of so-called landscape vocabulary. Since the words of landscape are physical, only so many can be fitted, quite literally, onto the site. Linguistic words, by contrast, take up no space and can go on indefinitely modifying and qualifying, even poeticizing. A similar problem arises from the metaphorical equation of rhetorical devices in language with rhetorical devices in the garden. Spirn has convincingly shown that both designed and un-designed landscapes employ rhetorical devices. But because of the physical nature of the landscape medium they employ only one or two at a time and not in the sort of strings that create arguments, as in written or spoken works. All too frequently a rhetorical device in landscape is a one-liner. Like a joke, a one-liner can point to a much larger issue, but it cannot express complicated ideas. For example, we get the point of Martha Schwartz's Splice Garden at a glance [figure 3-2]. Created for the Whitehead Institute for Biomedical Research, the garden, which is beautiful in its construction, suggests one response to the sort of research the institute performs. But it does not discuss it. For a knowledgeable audience the Splice Garden may also point to the origin of garden styles ("splice" serving as a metaphor for creative combination), but, again, it does not discuss the issue, a rather recondite one to be approached so broadly.

Now consider syntax: For the most part, designers achieve expression by deploying elements in addition (repetition) and juxta-position (contrast) of narrow and wide, enclosed and open, light and dark, hidden and revealed, high and low, smooth and rough, garden and setting, and so forth. They also have at their command miniatur-ization (or compression) and enlargement (expansion), both of which use contrast to a standard size to make their point. Writers and speakers express both repetition and contrast by the compound sentence. They express subordination, qualification, negation, and cause by the complex sentence. While it is possible for a garden designer to express subordination by placement, it is difficult—if not impossible—for the designer to show qualification, negation, and cause. For example, how would a designer make a complex-sentence version of the Splice Garden expressing the idea that although genetic engineering is ridiculous for gardens, it might be very useful for preventing certain diseases?

NATURAL MATERIALS AND CLAIMS TO MEANING

The expression of cause and effect is a particular problem for the garden, especially in the so-called "eco-revelatory" landscape, which purports to explain or express natural processes. For example, it has been said that George Hargreaves' landscapes express entropy. But since everything in the universe is under the sway of entropy, entropy would go on in Hargreaves' landscapes whether he chose to

3-2

MARTHA SCHWARTZ,
SPLICE GARDEN,
WHITEHEAD INSTITUTE FOR
BIOMEDICAL RESEARCH,
CAMBRIDGE,
MASSACHUSETTS, 1986.
[ALAN WARD]

express it or not. It is difficult, therefore, to read a Hargreaves landscape—without the written explanation—and know what is art and what is inevitable. The landscape is identical with the process it professes to express. We are reminded of the Nabokovian term paper in which the student explains that the trees in Jane Austen's novels express hope because they are green and green is the color of hope.

Such hindrances to garden meaning at first seem easily undone by exaggeration. For example, isn't it possible to express entropy— that is, show it as a cause—by hastening or exaggerating decay? Unfortunately, such a strategy looks just like careless construction and maintenance, a frequent and perhaps undeserved criticism of Hargreaves' landscapes. Well, then, what about expressing a process by exaggerating its opposite? But exaggerated maintenance does not remind us of entropy: So many gardens deny entropy by constant maintenance that it is all but invisible as an explanation. Similarly, couldn't designers express the life process of plants by growing them in media that kill them? The necro-revelatory garden would feature extensive plantings of large dying trees, which we could see had died because they were planted in, say, solid concrete. Such a garden could clearly express man's role in the death of plants, but in addition to running the risk of being labeled a one-liner and an installation rather than a garden, it would conceivably present no more than didactic information—how the palm tree does in concrete. After all, every garden is full of information that is embedded in its materiality. We do not even expect botanical gardens to have any meaning besides their classificatory information; generally it is the sort of information that requires a written label to make it available to us. Botanical gardens can, of course, be considered as evidence of social largesse as well as shifting cultural paradigms; but to be so considered they require a dedicatory plaque and even more explanatory labeling, perhaps provided by a social historian from a later historical era, what Laurie Olin calls "evolutionary" meaning.[13]

Scale also poses a representational problem in the eco-revelatory garden. Consider the Corn Garden: Plant a field of hybrid corn, the sort used to feed livestock. Make it two hundred miles square or make it ten feet square. In either case it is coterminous with a field of corn; it can give information about a field of corn, but it cannot give information about hybridization or the distribution system for animal feed in the United States because such information cannot be conveyed at the scale of a cornfield. Nor can the designer create a garden at the scale of hybridization or feed distribution. (A fence of cow skulls and grossly deformed corncobs?)

This hypothetical example shares the problem of many designed landscapes that concern themselves with water systems or wildflower ecology. They are stuck in being what they are.[14] Again, I do not mean to suggest that eco-revelatory landscapes are unpleasant or even uninformative to the already alerted and partially informed audience, but simply that they are ill-equipped to tell us anything we don't already know. Of course, these few examples do not exhaust the wonderfully flexible incorporeality of language or the delightfully rigid solidity of landscape, but they will suffice here to suggest some of the problems designers encounter when they try to express complicated ideas in physical landscapes.

SUBJECTIVISM AND THE PRODUCTION OF MEANING

While these problems of meaning arise from the intrinsically material nature of landscape, criticism has generated other difficulties, particularly in shifting the production of meaning from designers to the audience (in the parlance of landscape architecture, the users of the site). In current theory, the designer puts into motion a set of codes, thereafter elaborated by the audience, which is an active participant in creating the meaning of the text. Treib succinctly explains this joint creation while also pointing out the necessity for a homogenous and educated audience, a situation no longer existing in contemporary society.[15]

The idea that meaning is solely located in the mind of man, interestingly enough, found an early voice in landscape theory. Stephanie Ross, among others, has pointed out the eighteenth-century example of Uvedale Price and Richard Payne Knight's argument over the Picturesque. In *An Essay on the Picturesque*, Price, following the ideas elaborated in Edmund Burke's *Philosophical Enquiry into the Origin of Our Ideas of the Sublime and Beautiful*, located meaning in physical objects (small and smooth expressing beauty, large and rough the sublime, and so forth).[16] Knight, in *An Analytic Inquiry into the Principles of Taste*, pointed out Price's error as "seeking for distinctions in external objects which only exist in the modes and habits of viewing and considering them." Significance, Knight argued, lies in the association of ideas: "To a mind richly stored, almost every object of nature or art that presents itself to the senses, either excites fresh trains and combinations of ideas, or vivifies and strengthens those which existed before."[17] We have come to side squarely with Knight. What we call meaning lies in our associations—with a subsequent diminution of specific, complex meaning resulting from the very looseness and generality and uncontrollability of association, from what Knight describes as the "fresh trains and combinations of ideas."[18] It is only to the degree that a designer can control the initial code that the meaning of the artifact is saved from the illimitable associations of the reader.

When Spirn attributes the ability to use rhetorical devices to the un-designed landscape, we might wonder how an un-designed landscape can employ rhetorical devices. What she means is that the reader of the landscape can find these devices in the un-designed landscape—as indeed in anything else—for this theory turns the whole world into an array of possible texts. All landscapes can be read like novels or poems. But the idea that meaning inheres in the landscape itself is a dubious proposition, as is the notion that more of the meaning inheres in a specific landscape than in anything else to which the reader turns his freely associating mind. Unfortunately, a change in the producers of meaning from creator to perceiver in no way assures that the texts so created have any particular complexity. They may or they may not. The reader participates in creating meaning when reading Proust and a Hallmark card, but the two texts are quite different in the range and complexity of the associations that they set out to evoke. Similarly, John Dixon Hunt's reading of a Hallmark card is quite different from that of, say, ten-year-old Emmett Walker. For one thing, being some sixty years older, Hunt has a much longer memory stuffed with many more associations that can be stimulated by the sight of a Hallmark card.

The diffusion that occurs when the production of meaning shifts from the designer to the reader of the landscape emerges in a recent book of landscape theory, *Landscape Narratives: Design Practices for Telling Stories*.[19] The authors, Matthew Potteiger and Jamie Purinton, apply the terms of narratology to designed landscapes to help us read them as texts, discussing such practices as naming, sequencing, and revealing and concealing. The book usefully alerts us to the importance of unarticulated codes and interpretive communities in uncovering and/or creating meaning in landscapes that range from the Natchez Trace to a botanic garden. In so doing, Potteiger and Purinton tell a wealth of stories—so many, in fact, that in the book the stories overwhelm the artifacts. Everything can and does have a story to tell because telling stories is a ubiquitous human habit, a human means of perceiving, a human mental process that draws all material to itself. What place doesn't invoke someone's memories? What place hasn't engaged a designer or a client? What place doesn't have a theory of how it came to be? For that matter, what landscape

151 /

does not give evidence of its own historical and cultural contexts? Stories, we might say, love to have characters and plots, or to put it more accurately, people love characters and plots and put them together in stories that tend to shift from the artifact to the designer, the owner, the cultural context, and then back again. Sometimes stories enrich the artifactual experience, but just as frequently they rob it of depth and complexity.

A related problem in the creation of meaning is the current popularity among designers of the open symbol, that is, a symbol that seems to be significant while actually attracting a wide range of undifferentiated associations and interpretations. For example, historically we know that the members of a certain seventeenth-century French audience—or interpretive community—understood the meaning of the frogs in the Latona fountain at Versailles [figure 3-3]. They knew that the frogs referred to a story in Ovid's *Metamorphoses* about the Lycian peasants who refused to shelter the mother of Apollo and Diana. They also knew that the frogs referred to the rebellious subjects of the Fronde, who had risen up against Louis XIV in his youth.[20] We are thus in a position to know enough of the original meaning—from reading Ovid and the historical information about who knew what—to enjoy a complex view of those frogs. We know what they mean and what the seventeenth-century courtiers knew they meant— although such knowledge may not affect us very much emotionally. But what about the frogs in Martha Schwartz's Rio Shopping Center in Atlanta [figure 3-4]? Those frogs may nod to their Versailles ancestors, but they do not take part in any other clearly defined story. They are free to be whatever we please—one of the Egyptian plagues, a choir of those "lonely frog[s]" who "ain't got no home," an array of princes in disguise, or nothing at all besides visual elements.[21] I would suggest that this

3-3

JULES HARDOUIN MANSART,

LATONA FOUNTAIN,

VERSAILLES, FRANCE, 1689.

[MARC TREIB]

very openness makes Schwartz's frogs very pleasurable, but not well-suited to conveying meaning. This sort of symbol, added to an all-inclusive acceptance of association, may account for the broad-brush simplicity of many of the stories that Potteiger and Purinton find in the landscape, meanings so general as to amount to a dearth of meaning—although not necessarily a dearth of pleasure.

Throughout this section I have employed a device usually indicative of sloppy—or poetic—writing in order to make a point. Gardens, artifacts, un-designed landscapes, and so forth do not tell, desire, or express anything. Only humans can do that. Only humans can express and interpret and read, but Potteiger, Purinton, Spirn, and many other landscape theorists tend to complicate issues by jumping into poetic language that ascribes agency and consciousness to the inanimate element—as I myself do.

Personification of the artifact is part and parcel of our emotional desire to be at one with the physical universe (or nature), a symptom of our desire to move the creation of meaning away from our own self-conscious minds and make it an intrinsic aspect of the physical universe from which we feel so alienated. But such usage—when the critic is not really clear about who is saying what to whom—also reminds us of the absence of a particular and complex meaning. It encourages us to believe that the universe is transparent to us because we are part of it, a fallacy in the real world that is revealed by the continuing difficulty and ever-changing conclusions of scientific inquiry, but also a pleasure indulged within the protected realm of the garden. Within the garden we can abandon thought; outside the garden we must think about the world—and we must think about our thinking.

3-4

MARTHA SCHWARTZ,
RIO SHOPPING CENTER,
ATLANTA, GEORGIA,
1988.
[MARTHA SCHWARTZ]

MAKING STOURHEAD MEAN

As soon as the problem of meaning in the garden arises, so too does the eighteenth-century English landscape garden. Stephanie Ross remarks upon "the complex meanings gardens of the time conveyed, and the daunting demands they placed on viewers and interpreters."[22] Of these gardens, none is presumably so "daunting" in its meaning as Stourhead, the English landscape garden developed by Henry Hoare in the first half of the eighteenth century and frequently cited by garden theorists as a landscape fraught with meaning [figure 3-5]. Here, if ever there was one, is a garden with a cognitive component. It is instructive, however, to examine how a well-informed visitor to Stourhead deals with what this meaning means. Laurie Olin, a noted landscape architect and one of the best writers in the field, gives an intelligent reading of Stourhead in *Across the Open Field: Essays Drawn from English Landscapes*. His account, despite its intelligence, nevertheless suggests that the "daunting demands" of interpretation have been exaggerated. Olin devotes twenty pages to Stourhead, including several full-page black-and-white sketches. He covers the history of the Hoare family: the sources of their fortunes, their political and marital alliances. He then recounts the biography of Henry Hoare, including his literary tastes, his Grand Tour, and the deaths of his two wives and various children. Next he discusses the various influences on Hoare's gardening tastes. In these pages, Olin reveals that he has read a good deal, including the archival material accumulated by the National Trust, and that "off and on for two years" he "prowled around the grounds of Stourhead in different seasons."

Before offering "a brief synopsis of [the] contents and itinerary" of the garden, beginning with a chronological account of Hoare's building projects from 1744 to 1771, Olin summarizes the meaning, the cognitive element:

3-5

HENRY FLITCROFT,
THE TEMPLE OF FLORA,
STOURHEAD, ENGLAND,
1744–46.
[MARC TREIB]

> The whole ensemble was in some degree a memorial to the dead
> —in this case, the numerous family members mourned by Hoare—
> and a testimonial to the perseverance of the survivors: to the
> founding of a family dynasty and to English, Puritan, agrarian,
> mercantile, and cultural values. The unifying theme was that of
> the voyage of Aeneas and the Trojan survivors, their piety and
> trials that led to the founding of Rome. Particular passages and
> key images of the epic were selected, which related to Hoare's
> desire to establish an elegiac tone.

Olin then takes the reader on a tour around the lake, telling what he sees as well as the associated information that a well-informed eighteenth-century visitor would presumably possess, including a thorough knowledge of Virgil's *Aeneid* and Ovid's *Metamorphoses*. Olin intelligently explains how such landscape elements as the Pantheon or the steep stairs to the grotto or the statues within the Pantheon or the temple of Apollo relate to the various texts. For example:

> Again a physical device brings forth our consideration of the
> appeal of the tales of Hercules and Aeneas to Hoare and his
> generation of Christians in general, and the manner in which
> they could be read as parallels to or similes of the journey of
> the soul through life toward holiness, Christ, or heaven, and
> especially each of these heroes' trials and sojourns in Hades
> before their eventual triumph and return (or resurrection).[23]

We should note that at this point in his exegesis Olin is no longer describing the itinerary of Stourhead as he himself experiences it. Rather, he has slipped from a consideration of the landscape itself to historical information, a merging of his own knowledge of the site with information available to the eighteenth-century audience (or the first interpretive community). He

3-6

LAURIE OLIN,
SKETCH OF THE PANTHEON,
STOURHEAD, ENGLAND,
1974.

[COURTESY LAURIE OLIN]

briefly describes an element, then moves to a consideration of the cultural milieu, and so he continues for the rest of the itinerary.

Although Olin considers Stourhead a masterpiece and a treasure, he never actually articulates a personal reaction to the cognitive content of Stourhead, and we continue to wonder how its themes affect him. What does Laurie Olin really feel about founding a dynasty? about the Puritan virtues of farming? about the imperial destinies of Rome and England? We never doubt that he is enjoying the information about Stourhead that he has acquired. But what about Stourhead itself? Since Olin is an artist who sketches constantly, we do have some nonverbal evidence that shows how he reacted to Stourhead considered apart from information about Stourhead. Olin's ink drawings include a sketch of the front façade with two groups of trees (one old, one replanted), five grazing cows, and a burgeoning cloud formation; a one-page sketch of a ha-ha and several cows presumably redirected by its presence; a map of the house and its adjacent hamlet; and a double spread of the Pantheon, lake, and islands [figure 3-6]. All of these sketches are enjoyable, even informative, but here too we find nothing that really suggests how Olin responded to the cognitive content of Stourhead—except to note that he does not address it.

Certainly the amount of time we spend reading what Olin writes about Stourhead is in no way equivalent to the amount of time it takes to tour the garden, so we might wonder how the visitor to Stourhead spends the time left over from taking in the cognitive content: enjoying the beauty of the scene, we suspect, experiencing the weather, the sky, the joy of being outside in the real world.[24]

A final observation about Stourhead: In *What Gardens Mean*, Ross uses Stourhead to illustrate how interpretations of a landscape can differ from each other: In this instance, does the lake represent Lake Avernus or the sea? With this example, Ross wants to demonstrate that gardens can be complex enough to bring about disagreements over specific symbols, pointing out, however, that "it may seem that not that much turns on this particular dispute."[25] She reviews a few interpretations of Stourhead and then, devastatingly for a book so entitled, abandons conceptual meaning at Stourhead—and, it would seem, in the landscape generally:

> I agree that in a poetic or emblematic garden those features tied to the iconography...will not reward sustained interest, at least not in their limited meaning-bearing role. How often in walking the circuit at Stourhead can one profitably think of Aeneas and his journey to the underworld?

Ross further admits that, of all a garden's features, "we are most likely to tire of a garden's cognitive component, the meaning conveyed by its iconographic program."[26]

It is significant that we could not say this about repeated viewings of, say, a Claude landscape or repeated readings of *The Aeneid* or *The Metamorphoses* because in these instances there is very little besides the cognitive component that can engage us; even a purely formal aesthetic appreciation of the paintings or the poems would be difficult without a continuing consideration of the cognitive component.

I contend that Olin's and Ross's experience of this most meaningful of gardens is testimony to the fact that, in spite of its reputation for meaning, nothing at Stourhead is complex enough to demand very much attention—especially if we divorce the artifact from its historical information. Stourhead is full of possible associations and full of possible information, but, on the whole, what passes for meaning at Stourhead is really just one pleasant distraction after another. And so it should be. Indeed, a lot of what passes for meaning in the garden is really distraction from meaning—distraction, more specifically, from the conscious experience of ourselves as separate from what we call nature.

When visiting the garden our minds are occupied by a range of appealing information, what's growing well, for example. We are also distracted by solving the riddles of iconography as at Stourhead or Ian Hamilton Finlay's Little Sparta or Versailles. Although they tell us more than the frogs at the Rio Shopping Center, the frogs at Versailles occupy our brains without leading us into any unpleasant thoughts, for there is really nothing more restful to the mind than allegory, in which all the meanings are decided on ahead of time and require of the audience only recognition, another definite pleasure. "I get it!" we say, and we are pleased with ourselves, at least initially.

And then we can generally ignore the statues and temples and follies except for the formal aesthetic pleasure that they unfailingly give. The pleasure of solving puzzles may also account for the presence in gardens of mazes, giant chessboards, and relatively undemanding games like croquet. Perhaps the chief value of studies like Potteiger and Purinton's and Spirn's also lies in the posing of garden riddles. What fun it is to distinguish one narrative strategy or rhetorical device from another: Is that artificial rock synecdoche or metonymy? Is that bench a gathering strategy? Is that repeated planting of azaleas assonance or alliteration? Who is the hero of that fountain? What is the true significance of the garden's name? And so it is that while occupied in figuring out this and guessing about that, in observing one thing and wondering about another, the mind forgets that it has always believed—and feared—itself to be a thing apart from nature and, withdrawing into its happiness, annihilates the entire universe, itself included, to a green thought in a green shade.

NOTES

1 Marc Treib, "Must Landscapes Mean? Approaches to Significance in Recent Landscape Architecture," *Landscape Journal*, Number 1, 1995.

2 In trying to read a complex meaning expressed by a designer using physical garden elements, the user of a designed landscape faces a problem that reminds us of an older and even more difficult epistemological quandary: How do humans go about reading and understanding the physical universe? In this quandary, instead of questioning the expressive adequacy of the designer's means, we question our ability to perceive and understand: Can we escape the structures of the human mind in order to understand physical reality? This problem lies well beyond the scope of my essay, but two admirable studies of different modes of inquiry can be found in Thomas S. Kuhn, *Structure of Scientific Revolutions*, Chicago: University of Chicago Press, 1964, and Roberto Calasso, *Ka: Stories of the Mind and Gods of India*, New York: A. A. Knopf, 1998.

3 Although I hesitate to put too fine a point to this fantasy, we can imagine a similar scenario for gardeners in cultures that highly prize stones. For example, in the Heian period *Sakuteiki*, the term for gardening is *ishi wo taten koto*—translated as "the art of setting stones," *Sakuteiki: Visions of the Japanese Garden: A Modern Translation of Japan's Gardening Classic*, Jiro Takei and Marc P. Keane, translators, Boston: Tuttle Publishing, 2001. Another phrase, *ishi no kowan ni shitagahite*, translated as "follow the request of the stone," suggests that the stones are animate and have desires. Perhaps the garden in Japan and China began as a desire to merge human consciousness with stone, a material exploited for dams, walls, and terraces, important concerns in agricultural societies.

4 John Dixon Hunt, *Greater Perfections: The Practice of Garden Theory*, Philadelphia: University of Pennsylvania Press, 2000, p. 71.

5 Margery Fish, *We Made a Garden*, New York: Modern Library, 2002, pp. 96-97.

6 Ibid., p. 103.

7 Ibid., p. 118.

8 Clarence Glacken, *Traces on the Rhodian Shore: Nature and Culture in Western Thought from Ancient Times to the End of the Eighteenth Century*, Berkeley: University of California Press, 1967.

9 Treib, "Must Landscapes Mean?" pp. 89-93, 95. An amusing criticism of meaning-obsessed gardens can be found in Alex Martin and Jerome Fletcher's novel, *The Decadent Gardener*, which purports to record the landscape work of Medlar Lucan and Durian Gray at Mountcullen, the country seat of Mrs. Conchita Gordon. In this parody, the authors skillfully catch the tone of

the meaningful project description. Sawtry, U.K.: Daedalus, 1996.

10 For a brilliant but succinct explanation, see Rudolph Wittkower's 1966 essay, "Classical Theory and Eighteenth Century Sensibility," in *Palladio and English Palladianism*, New York: Thames and Hudson, 1983.

11 See Hunt's excellent explanation, which makes use of Michel Foucault and Svetlana Alpers, *Greater Perfections*, pp. 78–85. Hunt also devotes a chapter to words and images in the garden: "The primary function of words on a landscape architectural site would be to communicate certain kinds of meaning, including hints of a narrative," p. 119. Hunt does not consider the need to use words as evidence of failure on the part of the physical elements of the garden to convey meaning; the words, he points out, depend on the verbal skills of the visitors to the garden, which he implies may be weaker than their other interpretive skills. He nevertheless points out that garden experiences are "more often than not translated into linguistic expression," p. 128.

12 Ann Whiston Spirn, *The Language of Landscape*, New Haven: Yale University Press, 1998, p. 27. Spirn seems fitfully aware that her theory is based on metaphorical statement. For example, midway in the book she reminds the reader that "too close a comparison between verbal and landscape grammar must be resisted," p. 171.

13 Laurie Olin, "Form, Meaning, and Expression in Landscape Architecture," *Landscape Journal*, Number 2, 1988, p. 160.

14 In making this point in "Form, Meaning, and Expression in Landscape Architecture," Olin explains that "nature is the great metaphor underlying all art" and claims that designed landscape works "carry an expression of our ideas about nature and our place in the scheme of things." He includes a range of historical and contemporary examples and intelligently insists that "whatever meaning occurs in any landscape, natural or otherwise, is only that which has been created by society." A certain vagueness arises, however, when he comes to saying what various landscapes actually mean. Although he includes topics (healing in Central Park, "meditation on post-Civil War America" in Prospect Park, Gasworks Park as a "memento mori") and references to nature (Lawrence Halprin's two waterfalls, for example), he does not tell us the specific content of any of these topics or references. Conceivably he neglects the elaboration of general topics into specific comments because he ran out of space, or he may have realized that these landscapes don't elaborate their topics beyond the general statement. For example, what does Halprin actually say about waterfalls?

15 Still, Treib does not eliminate the possibility of meaning in the garden:

"Can a (landscape) designer help make a significant place? Yes. Can a (landscape) designer design significance into the place at the time of its realization? No, or let's say, no longer." Significance ultimately "lies with the beholder and not alone in the place," "Must Landscapes Mean?" p. 99. Hunt would agree, *Greater Perfections*, pp. 9ff.

16 Uvedale Price, *An Essay on the Picturesque*, London, 1794; Edmund Burke, *A Philosophical Enquiry into the Origin of Our Ideas of the Sublime and Beautiful*, James T. Boulton, editor, Notre Dame: University of Notre Dame Press, 1968.

17 Richard Payne Knight, *An Analytic Inquiry into the Principles of Taste*, London, 1805.

18 Stephanie Ross, *What Gardens Mean*, Chicago: University of Chicago Press, 1998, p. 136.

19 Matthew Potteiger and Jamie Purinton, *Landscape Narratives: Design Practices for Telling Stories*, New York: John Wiley, 1998.

20 Although this information is general, it is succinctly explained by Elizabeth Barlow Rogers in her textbook, *Landscape Design: A Cultural and Architectural History*, New York: Harry N. Abrams, 2001, p. 174.

21 *Ain't Got a Home* was recorded by Clarence "Frogman" Henry, circa 1973.

22 Ross, *What Gardens Mean*, p. 189.

23 Laurie Olin, *Across the Open Field: Essays Drawn from English Landscapes*, Philadelphia: University of Pennsylvania Press, 2000, pp. 264-265, 271.

24 The reader may gain additional insight, apropos the absence of meaning at Stourhead, from Lance Neckar's perceptive article about the meanings of Castle Howard, "Castle Howard: An Original Landscape Architecture," *Landscape Journal*, Number 1, 2000, p. 1. Neckar thoroughly studies the origin of the landscape and the subsequent reactions to it. Visitors (from several centuries) sensed significance but could elicit no specific meaning or, at best, gamely constructed a meaning after the fact. Neckar explains the functional origin of various design moves, chronologically orders the subsequently created meanings, and beautifully expresses the thought that Castle Howard "is predominantly self-referential," p. 41. Tom Williamson also warns that "the intellectual demands made on visitors to these gardens (Stowe, the Leasowes, Painshill, Stourhead) should not be exaggerated. The line between complex intellectual game, emotional stimulation, and cheap thrills is not always an easy one to draw in the English landscape garden," *Polite Landscapes: Gardens and Society in Eighteenth-Century England*, Baltimore: The Johns Hopkins University Press, 1995, p. 68.

25 Ross, *What Gardens Mean*, p. 73.

26 Ibid., p. 163.

Commentary 3:

_____

_____

Jane Gillette

REACHING THE TOPIC

Some years ago now, I went on a reading binge to catch up on tenth-
to eighteenth-century Chinese and Japanese novels retranslated in
the past twenty years. In these novels gardens are frequently used
as symbols for various social institutions like marriage and imperial
government or synecdoches of the culture as a whole. At about the
same time I visited a garden that I was told represented the history
of South Africa. Instead of the terrible, bloody history of that country
I saw three plant associations: Dutch, English, native. We all go
though life experiencing different sorts of artistic media, and even
though we don't expect or want them to do the same thing, we do
like to distinguish among them, not to rate them but to experience
them at their fullest. I found this difference between the fictional
and the real garden curious, and later I wrote what I thought of as
a footnote to Marc Treib's article "Must Landscapes Mean?"[1]

In my article I asked the question, Can gardens mean? And I answered that they cannot mean or they cannot mean much; that is, they are frequently one-liners that state a theme but don't develop it. I was pointing out that the weakness of the garden as a medium lies in the representation of ideas. I didn't write about the strength of the garden because I assumed, unwisely, that we all take that for granted. Here, let me state that I think the strength of the garden as an artistic medium is its celebration of actuality; that is, its ability to heighten our emotional experience of the actual material world and, in this heightened state, make us forget our persistent belief that we are separate from nature. The garden is what it is. It doesn't "mean." It "is."

CELEBRATION OF ACTUALITY

By means of skillful disposition and arrangement garden forms emphasize material actuality. This is the case wherever those forms come from: earlier gardens, other artistic media, agricultural experience, natural landscape, the mind of the designer, or the human mind in general.[2] Aided by these forms, we experience the garden with our physiological systems, a vast experiential effect—what Treib nicely calls "pleasure." Pleasure, which can be attained through a range of activities like maintaining, observing, and making, results from the impression that we are at one with actuality, with nature. Of course we really are part of nature, but we frequently don't feel that way because our minds seem to stand between us and the world. In the garden we are able to escape our minds and forget ourselves, a particularly valuable experience in a world that seems dominated by representations. In my article, I made a rather poetic statement about the human desire to feel that we are at one with nature, citing as evidence the frequency with which writers about gardens use the pathetic fallacy, a variety of personification that erases the difference between humans and nonhuman entities.[3]

When I visit a designed landscape I try to stay in the actuality that it celebrates. This experience can be put into words although, frankly, the resulting text sounds idiotic: Wow! What a tree! Isn't it terrific the way a row of trees shows how trees are similar, how different? Isn't it cool the way a flat plane of water reflects the sky? Isn't it amazing what a swan does to the surface of a lake? Why does flatness modify our perception of the sky? Isn't a slope an amazing thing? Et cetera. These perceptions are not a response to representations of ideas, what I have called meaning. They are responses to the thing itself, encouraged by various design strategies. A garden presents us with thousands upon thousands of these perceptions, which, no doubt, vary among the users of the site because of differences in cultural affiliations, historical period, and personal associations. Still, despite these differences, humans share a physiological system so there must be at least some similarity in our responses.

REPRESENTATION

As the obverse of this celebration of actuality, the garden is not an easy medium for the representation of ideas; this is true for the designer who is representing and for the user who is interpreting.[4] I mention both groups because representation involves, in fact is determined by, communication—communication that is always mediated by conventions (agreements between the maker and the user).

In my article I gave some reasons why I think it's so difficult to make a garden represent a complicated idea.

1. We are unable to tell the represented from the representation. (Laurie Olin intelligently addresses this in his essay as a problem of metaphor.)

2. There is no garden vocabulary and syntax that expresses such complicated intellectual constructions as: *but, maybe, not really, because.*

3. The conventions of the garden do not control narrative.

Even though the garden is not an easy medium for representation, it can take place. In my terminology gardens can "mean"—but not much. In other words, gardens are frequently one-liners that state but don't develop an idea. It's fun to speculate that the way we users react to these one-liners is conditioned by our desire to return as quickly as possible to the actuality that is the strength of the medium. Confronted by a garden one-liner:

1. We dismiss the idea as quickly as possible. For example, if the landscape at Stourhead asks me, "Is England the next Rome?" I think, well, I really must reread Book Six of *The Aeneid* sometime, or I wonder what Mr. Gibbon thinks about that. And, then, I dismiss the idea from my mind and set about enjoying actuality. I climb that hill and look at the follies from a different point of view. I run around and look at the specimen trees.

2. We appreciate the joke. Confronted with a postmodern Japanese garden in California, I laugh. And then I pay attention to the effect of natural rocks juxtaposed to manmade ripples of sand.

3. We try to understand the represented idea, but we dismiss it because we realize we cannot escape the specific intellectual world we inhabit. My favorite example of this rejection occurs in a novel by Italo Calvino. Mr. Palomar visits Ryoan-ji and is handed a piece of paper that explains what the garden "means": "If our inner gaze remains absorbed in the viewing of this garden we will feel divested of the relativity of our individual ego, whereas the sense of the absolute *I* will fill us with serene wonder purifying our clouded minds."[5] Mr. Palomar knows that he cannot bring his perceptions into line with this explanation because he is not a highly trained, well-read Zen Buddhist; instead he is a twentieth-century Italian with a skeptical mind alert to all sorts of nonsensical explanation. If I were handed this explanation at Ryoan-ji, I, too, would opt out and I would simply admire the sand, the rocks, the wall. If I were in a bad mood I would wonder why a true master of Zen Buddhism would need this garden to reach the "Absolute I." Why is Ryoan-ji unique or even

unusual for a Zen master? If he is capable of perceiving the "Absolute I," wouldn't he be able to do so in alleys? in garbage dumps? and in every garden, including Susan Herrington's non-Ryoan-ji?[6]

4. We are disappointed. For me such disappointment comes from a number of gardens because of:

a. *Linguistic nonsense*: I am told a garden represents somebody's idea of nature, and I am forced to worry about whether such a statement is a tautology when all I want to do is watch the swan. Or I am told that this garden is a narrative about water running downhill. All of us have flavored project descriptions with such statements, but they are irritating nonetheless.

b. *Easy irony*: This factory used slave labor to make instruments of war, but planting flowers in it reminds us that swords have been changed into ploughshares. I notice that such a strategy also disguises and diminishes a terrible history.

c. *Inadequate or deceptive information*: I am told that a mound "makes reference to" Indian mounds. I am irritated and ask, What Indians? Hopewell? Adena? Are they directional mounds? Burial mounds? Who are we to suppose is buried in them? Of course I like mounds per se because they look good against the sky and are fun to climb.

d. *Too much information*: The paths in a designed streetscape are made of different materials to show that they lead to historical buildings with different functions. Why? What is the point?

THEORY

It is a curious thing that no matter what the art, the discourse about the art takes place in large part in written language. In reading landscape theory I get the impression that many landscape academics believe the questions we have been discussing today were stated, addressed, and solved sometime in the mid-1980s, maybe at the Harvard Design School. Perhaps because I have been trained in literary history I believe that, despite small refinements, the issues addressed by theory are never solved. Far from proving anything, theory provides talking points for a conversation that is endlessly ongoing. Students need to be educated in these talking points because they will encounter the conversation for the rest of their lives.

In these articles we have touched on several important issues, including:

1. Where do garden forms come from?

2. Who is the controlling partner in artistic creation, the artist/designer or the perceiver/user?

As for the origin of forms: That conversation reaches backward at least to Plato and Aristotle. As for the artist/perceiver debate, for centuries this conversation has pleasantly oscillated between poles, that is, between statements of extreme positions—for example, the notion that the artist controls the idea or the counter position (Michel Foucault's notion) that the artist is an invention of the user community. Just in my reading lifetime, theory on this point has veered from the extreme artist-empowering statements of the New Criticism to the postmodern empowerment of the user in the 1970s. On the side of user-empowered theory, I think we have a great desire to eliminate the maker of the garden. For cultural evidence of this I cite the presence of thousands of gardens in novels, poems, paintings, and movies that are seldom accompanied by any garden makers. Perhaps we wish them absent because their existence imposes itself between the garden artifact and us, thus interfering with our desire to be at one with nature.

I am, nevertheless, uncomfortable with the idea that the more user-interpretations the better. Are they all that different? In every English course I've ever taught, a student inevitably declares that this poem, novel, story, whatever, can mean anything he/she wants it to mean. My inevitable answer: Of course it can, but why would it? We readers sometimes share a cultural history, and we always share a human history: that is, we share physiological and intellectual mechanisms, and it is within those common parameters that we

171 /

experience all artistic media. In this belief I reveal myself as a closet Structuralist.

Still, considering the arguments of artist-empowering theory, I know that whatever their claims to control, all artists employ conventions, those useful agreements between artist and audience. And I also know that artists manipulate these conventions in original and unique ways that keep power in their corner. It may be that we're oscillating back again, shifting a little from theories that validate the user toward arguments that validate the maker of the artifact. I've heard this theory called the New Aestheticism, but by any name it merely marks a stage, not a conclusion. The discussion will continue.[7]

NOTES

1 "Must Landscapes Mean? Approaches to Significance in Recent Landscape Architecture," *Landscape Journal*, Number 1, 1995.

2 Unlike Laurie Olin I enjoy garden materials like asphalt, plastic, and glass, for even if they are untraditional they are "actual." See "Form, Meaning, and Expression in Landscape Architecture," *Landscape Journal*, Number 2, 1988.

3 The pathetic fallacy attributes emotion, speech, and agency to non-human entities; since it blurs human agency, many critics find its use undesirable. By contrast I find the pathetic fallacy a positive expression of an understandable human desire to merge with nature.

4 A good article about the difficulty of representing an idea in a designed landscape is Julia Bryan-Wilson's "Building a Marker of Nuclear Warning," which deals with the struggle to mark a Waste Isolation Pilot Plant in New Mexico, in Robert S. Nelson and Margaret Olin, editors, *Monuments and Memory, Made and Unmade*, Chicago: University of Chicago Press, 2003.

5 Italo Calvino, *Mr. Palomar*, William Weaver, translator, New York: Vintage, 1985, p. 83.

6 Susan Herrington, "Gardens Can Mean," *Landscape Journal*, Number 2, 2007, p. 310.

7 In reading and commenting on each others' articles we have, consciously or not, relied heavily on the time-honored theoretical strategy of misprision. See Harold Bloom, *The Anxiety of Influence: A Theory of Poetry*, New York: Oxford University Press, 1973.

4.

Gardens Can Mean

Susan Herrington [2007]

In "Can Gardens Mean?" Jane Gillette writes: "my contention that the denial of meaning is an integral feature of the garden may at first seem startling. Actually, it is a notion more generally accepted than stated, one that can be detected in a range of evidence."[1] For Gillette, language better expresses meaning and "what passes for meaning in the garden is really distraction from meaning—distraction, more specifically, from the conscious experience of ourselves as separate from what we call nature."[2] Her question advances points made by Marc Treib in his article "Must Landscapes Mean?" in *Landscape Journal* some years earlier.[3] Both articles continue a trajectory of discussions concerning meaning that date back to Mark Francis and Randolph T. Hester, Jr.'s *The Meaning of Gardens* and Laurie Olin's "Form, Meaning, and Expression in Landscape Architecture" published in *Landscape Journal*.[4] While Francis, Hester, and Olin illustrate how gardens and landscapes have

4-1

ISAMU NOGUCHI, *CALIFORNIA SCENARIO*, COSTA MESA, CALIFORNIA, 1984.

[MARC TREIB]

meant, Treib is perplexed by designers and critics who think they should mean. On the other hand, Gillette questions the ability of gardens to mean at all.

What I find fascinating about the articles by Treib and Gillette is what they refer to as gardens and landscapes. For Gillette, gardens range from a meadow designed in a park, to frog fountains, to conventionally labeled gardens like Stourhead. For Treib, landscapes include fountains, plazas, memorials, and parks. Both authors admit that they will not define what they are writing about: landscapes and gardens. Perhaps they are nominalists—meaning that they do not believe that gardens or landscapes are defined by any real essences. It is likely that Gillette is an essentialist, since she consistently refers to "the garden" throughout her text as if there is a universal garden that we all share.

But if there is no common measuring stick by which we judge works as gardens or landscapes, perhaps these works must be addressed like Arthur Danto's ontology of art. Danto argues that art is defined by works that respond to a context or discourse about art, a discourse created by art critics, philosophers, and theorists.[5] Obviously, landscape architecture is not the New York art world; yet it does have a context of academics, practitioners, writers, and students who generate theories about landscapes and gardens, particularly through *Landscape Journal*. Both Gillette and Treib are distinguished writers and theorists. Landscapes and gardens highlighted by them, even ones no longer extant, are examples of landscape architecture that matter—to them, and thus, to landscape architecture. However, if we accept Gillette's proposition that gardens are devoid of meaning, then it becomes very interesting to know by what standards Gillette and Treib have constructed their critical canon.

Because Gillette's and Treib's speculations are philosophical, I have consulted the work of philosophers and historians who have grappled with the meaning of art for the past century. Gillette provides three main reasons why gardens cannot communicate, evident in the way (a) gardens are described by writers (particularly in their use of the "pathetic fallacy"); (b) the influences of postmodern culture on approaches to landscape design; and (c) how the physical medium of gardens make attributing meaning to them difficult. Therefore, I open my case with a discussion of the pathetic fallacy, showing that it is not a good indicator for determining if gardens can mean. This is followed by an assessment of Gillette's critique of postmodern culture. I highlight her omission of earthworks, which have inspired landscape architects to use their materials, context, and design strategies (such as narrative) as integral to the meaning of design. Then I address the medium of gardens, emphasizing that the physical elements of gardens can be shaped and composed by designers to communicate.

The second section of the essay concerns meaning itself and the inclusion of interpretation as a way of understanding meaning. I critique Gillette's version of meaning and attempt to clarify who authors meaning. I also assert that multiple interpretations do not dilute meaning and that the movement of our bodies, sensations, and emotions are part of meaning.

I. PATHETIC FALLACY

According to "Can Gardens Mean?" the use of pathetic fallacy to describe gardens is a symptom of their inability to mean.[6] The pathetic fallacy is the act of attributing emotions, thoughts, and aspirations to objects that could not possibly have these states of consciousness. The term originated with John Ruskin (1819–1900). In *Modern Painters III* Ruskin complained that Romantic-era artists who used the pathetic fallacy were self-indulgent and morally compromised.[7] According to Ruskin, artists who employed the pathetic fallacy in their artful descriptions of objects were actually denying these objects their ability to elicit sensations directly. For example, Ruskin condemned poets who described a primrose as a star or a fairy's shield, but condoned a poet who "perceives rightly in spite of his feelings, and to who the primrose is forever nothing else than itself—a little flower."[8] Ruskin's critique is dubious. For example, Dorothy and William Wordsworth's literary references to daffodils dancing and laughing do not semantically disable the daffodils planted in their garden at Dove Cottage. In other words, their use of pathetic fallacy does not inhibit the physical daffodils' ability to mean.

Gillette, however, does not find the desire to ascribe human traits to elements in gardens a moral error. In contrast to Ruskin, it is the inability of gardens to intend that forces authors to resort to a set of anthropocentric metaphors to describe them. Ruskin's theory hinges on his belief that daffodils express something as daffodils, while "Can Gardens Mean?" argues that a daffodil is unable to express anything. In light of this, Gillette argues that the use of pathetic fallacy indicates our desire to be part of unconscious nature:

> [P.]ersonification of the artifact is part and parcel of our emotional desire to be at one with the physical universe (or nature), a symptom of our desire to move the creation of meaning away from our own self-conscious minds and make it an intrinsic aspect of the physical universe from which we feel so alienated.[9]

As argued in "Can Gardens Mean?" when we assign human qualities to garden elements we attempt to be reconnected to a past when we were one with nature. Gillette admits that it is difficult to verify the relationship between our Paleolithic or Neolithic ancestors and nature. Nonetheless, if the pathetic fallacy is employed to be part of unconscious nature, this does not mean the garden is bereft of meaning. In fact, I don't think the pathetic fallacy is a way of connecting to external nature at all, but to people.

Some theorists think that the projection of emotions onto the external world allows for a shared space to be created between the reader and artist through the object of art.[10] It enables the reader to understand the human emotions of another through an experience with the work, carving out a reality that humans share. This act does not compromise the meaning of the work, even if it is a garden. For example, the pathetic fallacy was not common in modern poetry but, as Gillette notes, women writers used it frequently in the early twentieth century.[11] In "Cultivating Power: The Language of Feminism in Women's Garden Literature, 1870–1920" Dianne Harris found that women's garden literature was written in the form of lore rather than in scientific language associated with the male expert.[12] By developing a separate culture of writing and gardening these women sought to simultaneously define and empower themselves in regard to real property, traditionally the domain of male authority.

While Harris does not mention the use of pathetic fallacy, it does appear in some of the writing she features. For example, in "My Flowers," Sophia Johnson writes:

A flowery crown will I compose,
I'll weave the Crocus, weave the Rose;
I'll weave Narcissus, newly wet,
The Hyacinth and Violet;
The Myrtle shall supply me green,
And Lilies laugh in light between,
That the rich tendrils of my darling's hair
May burst into their crowning flowers,
and light the painted air.[13]

While disguised as a poem, Johnson is actually describing to readers the composition of flowers in her garden. Here, the use of the pathetic fallacy is a way to communicate to other women using the language they all know, Romantic verse. So there is good reason to suppose that the use of pathetic fallacy by these women writers was actually aimed at connecting with each other as non-experts. After all they are writing to each other, not to nature. Men also used pathetic fallacy, but again, I think this was a way to garner their identity as a type of gardener.

POSTMODERN PROBLEMS

Another theme in "Can Gardens Mean?" is a critique of postmodernism even though postmodernist analyses could help secure an argument against meaning. Instead, postmodern culture is presented as an accomplice in our eagerness to make gardens mean. As a lead-in to suspicions about postmodern culture, Gillette uses Treib's critique of postmodern landscapes in "Must Landscapes Mean?." Treib cautions that in their quest to give meaning to landscapes, designers are overlooking the importance of pleasure and human comfort. We know from his widely read book, *Modern Landscape Architecture: A Critical Review*, that modern landscapes were designed for people's comfort and use.[14] This was one of the tenets of modern landscape design. In fact, the great modernist landscape architect Garrett Eckbo (1910–2000) declared in his classic *Landscape for Living* that landscape design is a "conscious rearrangement of the elements of the landscape for use and for pleasure."[15]

Yet Treib finds this emphasis on people's use and pleasure blatantly absent from many of the postmodern landscapes he discusses. For example, he notes that Isamu Noguchi's *California Scenario* (1984) in Costa Mesa, California, fails to provide the basic amenity of shade [figure 4-1]. *California Scenario*'s blurring of sculpture and landscape, its use of narrative and resistance to solving site problems such as microclimatic conditions, are commonly cited features of postmodern landscapes. As its title suggests, *California Scenario* was intended to evoke the California landscape and some of its major geographic features—forests, waterways, and mountains. Treib experiences *California Scenario* as hot and sunny. Southern California on many days is hot and sunny. Noguchi is expressing this in his scenario, not solving the problems of the plaza being too sunny and hot. Treib concludes that the desire to ascribe meaning in postmodern landscapes is a reaction to modernist landscape architects' rejection of history. Indeed, postmodern landscapes like *California Scenario* revive an historical design strategy, the narrative. However, I think it is reasonable to assume that landscapes can employ narrative as a design strategy and also provide comfort. Consider the numerous Italian Renaissance gardens that offer narratives as well as a comfortable respite from the hot climate.

In addition to comfort, Treib finds that sensory experience is also missing from many postmodern landscapes. After a witty diagnosis of the numerous ways that designers have attempted to make their landscapes mean, he asks: "Could we not make the place pleasurable?"[16] These are not mutually exclusive properties. Interpretations of landscapes can be pleasurable, but Treib argues that landscape architects should be less concerned with ascribing meaning to their landscapes and more concerned with creating landscapes that are pleasurable to all the senses. Certainly designers can intend their gardens to communicate but they can also give great pleasure to the users as part of their meaning.

Treib's example of the Tanner Fountain by Peter Walker is a good case in point [figure 4-2]. Treib writes that Walker's design makes subtle references to *Stone Field Sculpture*, a 1977 public artwork in New Hartford, Connecticut, by minimalist artist Carl Andre (1935–). For Treib, "from sculpture, the designer receives both the instigation of ideas and, to some degree, of validation."[17] This is believable, and consistently supported by Walker's own account. Walker admires minimalist art, and as Rosalind Krauss predicted, minimalism proved to be one of the most significant art movements of the twentieth century. These artists were interested in meaning as well, particularly in the way it is generated in a public space, so this is an appropriate art form for public landscapes to model.[18]

Both *Art on File* and The Center for Urban and Regional Policy at Northeastern University include the Tanner Fountain in their lists of Boston's public art—so Walker has presumably been successful.[19] Nonetheless, it is significant to note that Tanner Fountain is one of the most popular outdoor spaces on the Harvard campus—even in winter. During the summer months you are lucky to find a rock to sit on—and there are 159 of them. It is comfortable and viscerally pleasurable. The rocks are seats for adults to sit on and study or socialize. For children, they are mountains and the grass is a sea of giant child-eating lizards. It is simultaneously meaningful, comfortable, and pleasurable—and this is a result of Walker's specific design.

Adding to Treib's insights, Gillette identifies three influences of postmodern culture and our quest to make gardens mean. These influences are (1) the role of craft and anti-consumer rhetoric; (2) a veritable food chain of intellectual legitimization in which landscape architects copy architects who copy literary critics who copy artists who copy philosophers; and (3) that the increasing use of words by "the audience" in relation to gardens has intensified concerns with producing and controlling meaning.[20] Missing from this list of symptoms is the profound role that earthworks, minimalism, and public art have played in shaping how gardens can mean. Works by artists like Robert Smithson, Mary Miss, Ian Hamilton Finlay, and Mags Harries inspired landscape architects to approach their projects with concerns beyond accommodating the requirements of a project's program. Books about this art—e.g., *Earthworks and Beyond* by John Beardsley and *Between Landscape*

4-2

PETER WALKER / SWA GROUP,
TANNER FOUNTAIN,
HARVARD UNIVERSITY,
CAMBRIDGE, MASSACHUSETTS,
1984.
[MARC TREIB]

Architecture and Land Art by Udo Weilacher—have also influenced the composition of gardens and landscapes and thus the way they communicate.[21]

The artists and designers described in these books share a similar palette of materials with landscape architects: terrain, water, sun, shadow, plants, rocks, concrete, manufactured objects, etc. However, they employ this material to express ideas. For Weilacher "material becomes the medium which influences the figurative and symbolic message of the work."[22] In response some landscape architects explored the communicative power of materials. In numerous gardens Martha Schwartz, Ken Smith, and Claude Cormier argue for a broader exploration of materials that are contemporary to our own times. For Schwartz the medium of landscape itself becomes the contested ground where the typical materials used by landscape architects are challenged. Similarly, Alexandre Chemetoff questions the traditional role that landscape has played in disguising technology and infrastructure although it is dependent upon it. In his Bamboo Garden at Parc de la Villette in Paris he exposes and incorporates the sewers, water mains, and electrical lines as part of his design, instead of camouflaging them [figure 4-3].

Many postmodern art movements, such as earthworks and site-specific art, defy the conventional art object placed in the museum by creating works that are integral to their location. An aspect of these movements that should not be underestimated is their preoccupation with context as an important evocation of meaning. Consider Beardsley's definition of earthworks: "their physical presence in the landscape itself distinguishes them from other, more portable forms of sculpture…Most of these works are inextricably bound to their sites and take as a large part of their content a relationship with the specific characteristics of their particular

4-3

ALEXANDRE CHEMETOFF,
BAMBOO GARDEN,
PARC DE LA VILLETTE,
PARIS, FRANCE, 1989.
[MARC TREIB]

surroundings."[23] Like these works gardens accrue meaning through their context as well. Narrative has become a common strategy for postmodern landscapes because narrative can account for context in ways that simply making a place comfortable does not.

Consider Claude Cormier's design for the Place d'Youville, a boulevard in an historic area of Montreal [figures 4-4, 4-5]. Although the design brief required accommodations for pedestrians along the grassy median of the boulevard, Cormier chose to design the pathways to communicate something more about the nature of the historical buildings that flank either side of the boulevard. Pathways connect the doorways of the buildings across the median, signaling to users the presence of these old structures, their facades, and the tapestry of entryways that open to this public space. In this way, the pathways signal a narrative. The materials Cormier selects to create the pathways also tell us something about the uses of these buildings. Wood is used for paths connecting to residential structures, while more enduring materials such as granite are used for links to official structures. There are also benches for sitting and mature trees to provide shade. It is a very comfortable place to sit, mentally connecting the pathways with the various doorways, façades, and their histories, and watching people. The paths also invite people to utilize the conventionally empty boulevard median. During the day people use the paths to enter the space at various points and in the evening musicians and other entertainers occupy the different paths. Thus, returning to Treib's point, garden designs that employ narratives can be comfortable while also accommodating varied uses.

4-4

CLAUDE CORMIER
ARCHITECTES PAYSAGISTES
+GROUPE CARDINAL HARDY,
PLACE D'YOUVILLE,
MONTREAL, QUEBEC,
MASTER PLAN, 1997.
[CLAUDE CORMIER]

4-5

CLAUDE CORMIER
ARCHITECTES PAYSAGISTES
+GROUPE CARDINAL HARDY,
PLACE D'YOUVILLE,
MONTREAL, QUEBEC, 2002.
[COURTESY DENIS FARLEY]

THE MEDIUM OF GARDENS

Marc Treib provides a definition of meaning, suggesting that it "comprises ethics, values, history, affect, all of them taken singly or as a group."[24] Jane Gillette finds this definition unmanageably broad, because it offers:

> no subject, no area of significance, that could only be expressed by the garden. Behind this observation lies my critical assumption that every medium champions itself; so that if people make gardens to express ideas, we need to ask what ideas the garden requires for its full and best expression that cannot be adequately achieved by some other medium.[25]

However, artists and designers have challenged the purity of the medium ever since the modern system of arts was categorized, between 1680 and 1830. According to historian Larry Shiner this system of arts initially included poetry, painting, sculpture, architecture, and music, with dance, rhetoric, and landscape gardening added by the late seventeenth century.[26] With the rise of formalist aesthetics critics stressed the purity of the medium within these categories, supporting the best-expression theory advanced by Gillette. However, movements and people as diverse as the Bauhaus, Walter Benjamin, Andy Warhol's factory, and the earthwork artists sought to make these categories more porous. Many categories of art were challenged because they were unable to fully account for our current world of mass production, digital media, and cultural difference. Perhaps both the purity of medium and the blending of artistic practices are social constructions. As Shiner contends:

> The modern system of art is not an essence or a fate but something we have made. Art as we have generally understood it is a European invention barely two hundred years old. It was preceded by a broader, more utilitarian system of art that lasted over two thousand years, and it is likely to be followed by a third system of arts. What some critics fear or applaud as the death of art

and literature or serious music may only be the end of a particular social institution constructed in the course of the eighteenth century.[27]

Adhering to the purity of eighteenth-century categories of art is limiting at best and can be as oppressive as other categories of Western culture—such as black or white, art or craft, fake or authentic, and male or female.

Even if we could transport ourselves back to a formalist heyday when each art was faithful to its essential medium, then what would be the medium of gardens? The list of garden elements—"water in the form of lakes, rivers, and fountains; paving of all sorts; walls, benches, statuary; grading; follies that range from grottos to temples; and flower, trees, stones, and shrubs"—is not sufficient to describe "a medium" of gardens. They don't suggest a medium in the same way that the medium of painting is "paint on canvas."[28] However, the critical assumptions regarding best medium are seriously weakened by the contention that gardens are unable to mean because garden elements themselves cannot communicate.

The argument is threefold. First, it is stated that gardens cannot mean because their elements are identical to what they are. Gillette writes, "in experiencing physical landscapes it is frequently difficult to distinguish between the artifact and the meaning of the artifact," and later finds fault with eco-revelatory landscapes.[29]

They are stuck in being what they are. Again, I do not mean to suggest that eco-revelatory landscapes are unpleasant or even uninformative to the already alerted and partially informed audience, but simply that they are ill-equipped to tell us anything we don't already know.[30]

According to this theory, rocks in a garden are inexpressive because they have not been sculpted into something else, or wildflowers cannot mean because they are in a garden rather than a painting. This contention ignores the role of art in garden design, architecture, sculpture, ceramics, weaving, and the last century of art theory. The notion that art is an imitation of real things in the world (called mimesis), and thus it cannot also be these real things in the world has been challenged by a century of artists such as Marcel Duchamp and Cindy Sherman as well as philosophers from John Dewey to Arthur Danto.

Referring to *What Gardens Mean* by Stephanie Ross, it's important to note the cornerstone of this philosopher's argument.[31] Drawing together the aesthetic theories of Suzanne Langer, Richard Wollheim, and Arthur Danto, Ross distinguishes between the physical world of gardens as pieces of land and the virtual world of gardens that are "the sensory experiences of (triggered by) its physical base."[32] For Ross, the perception of the physical and the virtual aspects of a garden are simultaneous. Garden elements are shaped and arranged by the designer, but their presence and design triggers our interpretation of them. Nonetheless, Gillette writes "gardens, artifacts, undesigned landscapes, and so forth do not tell, desire, or express anything. Only humans can do that."[33] This is akin to stating that the book of poetry sitting on my desk is simply a bound pile of paper impressed with ink, and does not communicate anything. Humans express ideas to other humans through the physical world, whether ink and paper, paint and canvas, or mud and stone.

When gardens are designed by humans as a medium to communicate ideas and emotions, they become the conveyance of expression. For example, in a hypothetical version of Gillette's Ryoan-ji garden, the rocks are rocks [figure 4-6]. Putting aside the wide range of associations that have been attributed to the Ryoan-ji rocks, if we believed "Can Gardens Mean?"

4-6

RYOAN-JI,
KYOTO, JAPAN, c. 1500.
[SUSAN HERRINGTON]

4-7

SUSAN HERRINGTON,
RYOAN-JI RECONFIGURED,
2007.
[SUSAN HERRINGTON]

and if the rocks were moved and placed in a line rather than in specific clusters, the garden would still be the same. Likewise, if the rocks themselves were manipulated, for instance, scrubbed clean of moss, it would be no different because the garden's rocks are rocks and can not mean anything other than a massing of hard consolidated mineral matter. Yet, because these manipulations would significantly change the way this garden communicates the intention of its designers, the rocks—their placement and their treatment—must be contributing something to how and what Ryoan-ji means.

There is also the influence of a viewer's perceptual engagement that allows gardens to operate as vehicles for meaning. It is true that eighteenth-century philosophers strengthened the role of the viewer in creating meaning from experiences, but this does not suggest that gardens and other works thereby lack the ability to express. In fact, by strengthening our abilities to read landscapes it makes us pay closer attention. The philosopher Dominic Lopes uses the term "design seeing" to account for the viewer's seeing paintings as paintings, or in our case gardens as gardens. Regarding pictures, Lopes states that design seeing "comprises the surface configurations that you see when you see the picture surface without seeing anything in it and that are responsible for your seeing something in it."[34]

Cultivating this regard is precisely the way we guide students of landscape architecture to read landscapes. It is helpful because reading the design takes into account the act of design and how design shapes interpretation. For Lopes, not every aspect of a design will feature in the viewer's cognition of it as a work. Returning to Ryoan-ji, for example, very subtle changes to the rocks—such as replacing one of the rocks with another similar looking rock in its exact location—will not change Ryoan-ji's ability to express. To me, the placement of these rocks suggests a series of rocky islands in a sea; to others the rocks represent a tiger and her cubs crossing the ocean. If these rocks were placed in a single row, I would not have made this interpretation, so the composition of the rocks must be telling me something [figure 4-7].

Linked to the problem of representation is the charge that it is often difficult to distinguish between "the container of meaning and the contents" in gardens.[35] Gillette finds that the strength of a Zen temple garden "lies in a clear demarcation of the container," while the gardens we might encounter in daily life are perhaps incapable of stirring our cognitive powers.[36] I agree that the contained space of a Zen temple garden like Ryoan-ji begs for interpretation. Also, its scale provides a useful example for determining the relationship between design and interpretation as demonstrated earlier. Unfortunately, there seems to be a need for the walls of a museum, the covers of a book, the frames of a painting to signal the mind to gear up for some serious brain-bending interpretation. In fact, Anne Whiston Spirn's contention that we can interpret non-designed landscapes and imbue them with meaning is critiqued "for this theory turns the whole world into an array of possible texts."[37]

Is it not better for people to have meaning in their daily lives? Should we find meaning only by traveling to Zen gardens and museums? In *Art as Experience*, the philosopher John Dewey argued that art should contribute meaning in everyday life, and not be locked up in a museum. Complaining that "objects that were in the past valid and significant because of their place in the life of a community now function in isolation from their conditions of their origin," Dewey aimed to recover "the continuity of aesthetic experience in the normal processes of living."[38] Since he was not concerned with the nature of art objects (he thought that rug-making could offer aesthetic experiences) and he stressed that aesthetic experience should be social rather than psychologically internal, many of his theories were rejected by the modern art world. However, his theories have recently been invigorated. Certainly, given the presence of gardens and landscapes in people's daily lives and their frequent use as social spaces, this makes them ideal locations for meaning.

II. WHAT IS IT TO MEAN?

"When I talk about the construction of meaning," Gillette writes, "I am not talking about the intervention of the human mind (which of course is involved in the design of gardens), but rather about the intervention of discursive reasoning, primarily language."[39] From this we may construe that the types of meaning carried in language— the system of words or conventional symbols that, when combined according to some type of grammar, enable us to communicate. "Can Gardens Mean?" thus implies that legitimate meaning should offer a singular, complex—content communicated through language by the author to the reader. However, several points remain to be clarified: Who are the authors of meaning? Can multiple meanings be legitimate? How do we actually derive meaning from gardens? The following section proposes a more modest, but inclusive version of meaning that accommodates these issues.

WHO AUTHORS MEANING?

"Can Gardens Mean?" relies too heavily on an understanding of meaning that is formulated by the designer and read by the user. Traditionally, art critics have relied on the artist's own declared intentions as the correct and proper meaning of a work of art. If the artist were dead, the work's meaning was gleaned through a hypothetical biographical explanation. This type of sleuthing into an artist's life story is similar to the way Laurie Olin aligns Henry Hoare II's personal life with the garden he created at Stourhead. In his eloquent comparison of Hoare's own life with that of Virgil's protagonist Aeneas, we are given an account of the way Stourhead was intended to mean for Henry Hoare II.[40]

But we also know from recent theories of art, from feminist interpretations to psychoanalysis, that the artist's intentions are not necessarily the correct interpretation of a work.[41] For example, Griselda Pollock argued that a male painter's interpretation of his work might only account for a male's interpretation of the world. Referring to two canonical paintings by Edouard Manet, *Olympia* (1863) and *A Bar at the Folies-Bergère* (1881–1882), Pollock asks, "How can a woman relate to the viewing positions proposed by either of these paintings? Can a woman be offered, in order to be denied, imaginary possession of Olympia or the barmaid?"[42] Thus, in feminist interpretation, some barriers may actually prevent people from interpreting a work as the artist envisioned.

Added to this critique of the artist's lock on meaning was an attack on the actual notion of an author itself. Michel Foucault revealed the elusive authority of artists in his famous article "What is an Author?"[43] Foucault argued that the author is not a person but something invented by a group, culture, society, or discipline (in our case, landscape architecture) to regulate discourse and ironically inhibit the creative freedoms of the human author. For Foucault, the author George Hargreaves in landscape architectural discourse is not the tall guy with curly hair. "Hargreaves" represents a certain category of landscape architectural practice that functions to regulate discourse about landscape architecture. Foucault's contention that the author is something formulated and controlled by discourse also weakens the older critical tradition that posited the artist's intent as the correct meaning of a work.

Yet, according to "Can Gardens Mean?" we must recognize the meadow as a garden by Andropogon Associates to find meaning in it. With an illustration of Andropogon's meadow of native grasses and wildflowers at Avalon Park, Gillette states that a person might visit the meadow and never guess "that something meaningful was afoot. This unconsciousness is part of Andropogon's design intent."[44] Andropogon may have intended not to communicate any cognitive content, but then why call it a "meadow," particularly given the conceptual and poetic resonance of meadows from Virgil to Robert Frost. More importantly, the users of Avalon Park might attribute all types of meanings to the meadow. For a scientist or landscape architect well acquainted with plant life and succession, this meadow will be loaded with cognitive content.

ONE MEANING OR MANY?

To determine how gardens can mean, we need to consider different perspectives involved in constructing meaning(s) from gardens: the users of the garden, the designer(s), and the critics. They all have variable intentions; from a single garden they will likely mine different meanings that are rarely communicated by written words. Conventionally it is the critic who writes about the meaning of gardens. Because landscape architecture magazines serve an educational role for practitioners, academics, and students, they often cite a designer's intentions in employing certain forms, materials, or spaces. However, these intentions are not presented as the only correct meaning. Instead, by revealing the intent and meaning of a garden from the designer's perspective, others may be inspired to consider similar approaches.

For many landscape architects the users of gardens offer the best interpretation. Empirical studies that ask people what they think about the landscapes they live in often make a valuable contribution. While these studies cannot, nor should they, account for the vast range of decisions that must be addressed in the design process, they provide a glimpse of how gardens mean to people in daily life. The non-professional may not interpret a garden the way a designer intended, but this does not render the garden meaningless. Rather, it suggests the garden possesses multiple meanings. There is a great deal to learn about the human imagination in comparing different interpretations, particularly in public spaces. Robert Riley stressed this point in his essay in *The Meaning of Gardens*:

> *Some meanings will turn out to be shared and reinforced. Others will not. But the first job of the designer is to think about what meaning he or she intends to convey in a design, and to be explicit about it. We can at least, then, learn from our failures and our successes in communication.*[45]

Assuming that landscapes have multiple authors leaves us with many meanings, perspectives, and viewpoints. An underlying thesis of "Can Gardens Mean?" seems to be that the author/designer delivers a singular, stable, yet complex meaning available to be interpreted by a dutiful reader. The past fifty years have witnessed radical transformations in the relationship between language and interpretation. Loosely labeled post-structuralism, and involving a range of thinkers and movements, these transformations have included the shift from a singular truth determined by the author to an emphasis on the multifaceted readings of language in the construction of meaning. Since the meaning we take from things is culturally constructed, it is unstable, like language, and subject to multiple interpretations or meanings. Postmodern critics and philosophers continue to stress the instability of meaning, but also the increased role of the reader in assigning meaning as part of the multifaceted nature of meaning.

While the author of "Can Gardens Mean?" is troubled by the number of stories in *Landscape Narratives*, it is the inclusion of many stories that gives the landscape importance.[46] The authors offer an approach to working with people whose stories are often excluded from the conventional site-analysis process practiced in landscape architecture. Through interviews and conversations with people about the landscapes they inhabit, Matthew Potteiger and Jamie Purinton demonstrate how people's personal stories can contribute to greater control over their environment, from stopping unwanted new landscapes to reclaiming old ones. Although these are narratives that you may not find in official documents or at the library they certainly exist in the minds of people nevertheless—and they are part of the way landscapes mean. Multiple meanings may shatter the idea of a singular reading prescribed by the author, but the inclusion of many interpretations may allow a more generous understanding of the meaning of gardens.

"Can Gardens Mean?" defends verbal and written language as the superior vehicle for delivering meaning, but this assumption should be revisited. In a critique of Anne Whiston Spirn's *The Language of Landscape*, Gillette asserts "it is, however, this very lack of fusion that makes verbal language such a useful tool for conveying meaning. A word or a formula is never the same thing as what it represents, so it cannot be mistaken for it."[47] Yet they are conditionally mistaken for what they represent, particularly when the objects they refer to are not present. Likewise, we agree as a culture of a language to mistake them for what they mean. We must mistake meanings for words every day in order to efficiently communicate. For instance, the letters *d-o-g* have nothing to do with the furry creature sitting at my feet right now—other than the fact that people speaking English have agreed to refer to him as a dog.

III. HOW GARDENS MEAN

"Can Gardens Mean?" searches for a complex meaning in gardens that is akin to interpreting great literature. Gillette stresses further the superiority of written words, speculating that complex meaning is more suited to written words than gardens because "words of landscape are physical, only so many can be fitted, quite literally on one site. Linguistic words by contrast, take up no space and can go on indefinitely modifying and qualifying, even poeticizing."[48] However, complex meaning cannot be directly tied to size or length. One can write at length and say very little; conversely, the shortest poems or even one line in a poem can offer complex meaning. This can be applied to gardens as well. Duration is another factor. People rarely read a book more than twice, yet gardens—particularly if they are in a residential location—can be experienced for decades. The duration of time that can be spent experiencing a garden makes available meaning through memory. This is a process that can lead to a garden having great significance, a point stressed by Treib.

The conclusion of "Can Gardens Mean?"—that gardens are not the best medium for delivering complex meaning—is based on a notion of meaning that is received optically and interpreted intellectually. Throughout "Can Gardens Mean?" a Cartesian nativism that lingers in the garden—a "conscious man" who is separate from his body. In fact the non-cognitive contents of gardens are often regarded as distractions but not as part of their meaning. For example, the assessment of Stourhead notes "certainly the amount of time we spend reading what Olin writes about Stourhead is in no way equivalent to the amount of time it takes to tour the garden, so we might wonder how the visitor to Stourhead spends the time left over from taking in the cognitive content: enjoying the beauty of the scene, we suspect, experiencing the weather, the sky, the joy of being outside."[49] This mind-body dualism not only excludes unconscious contributions to meaning but also the way sensorial experiences contribute to cognitive interpretations.

Treib, on the other hand, stresses that sensory experiences can contribute to meaning, writing:

In the past, sensory pleasures have served to condition meaning. Consider the expression of taste in the selection and arrangement of cut flowers in Japan or the ecstasy of religious experience that underwrote so much Counter-Reformation art and architecture. Sensory experience moved the viewer, causing him or her to reflect upon religious meaning as well as one's position in the universe—powerful stuff indeed.[50]

If we could reevaluate the way Gillette interprets (just as we revised the idea of who interprets, and the number of interpretations), we might then include other sensorial information received by the rest of the body in the construction of meaning. In doing so, gardens may be regarded as superior vehicles for meaning.

We know from developmental psychologist Jean Piaget (1896–1980) that sense experience is the primary source for our conceptual knowledge and the foundation blocks of meaning in developing children.[51] Neurological studies concerning the biological foundations of consciousness in adults have also found that our senses contribute to rational thought, challenging the Cartesian doctrine that knowledge cannot be derived from sensation. Neuroscientists have demonstrated that our brains are not locked in a bottle and that sensory experiences are a necessity for conscious man. Antonio Damasio has advanced the idea that cognition is the work of the entire body through "somatic markers."[52] These markers form the basis of human consciousness as they index sensations coming in from the external world that interact with cognitive representations of the internal world.

Thus, in addition to sight, sensual experiences are an important source for our conceptual knowledge and the foundations of meaning. Since gardens are most frequently outside, they can be intense sensorial environments with changing temperature, light, smell, and wind. In addition, the movement of our bodies through a garden can be a powerful agent for meaning. Unfortunately, the conscious human in "Can Gardens Mean?" does not move around the garden either, which is an integral

4-8

MICHAEL ARAD AND PETER WALKER, WORLD TRADE CENTER MEMORIAL, NEW YORK, NEW YORK, 2015. [PETER WALKER PARTNERS]

part of experiencing and interpreting gardens. Gillette contends that "we know from outside knowledge that the path from the gate to the door of a traditional Japanese teahouse has a spiritual dimension, but we cannot know that simply by looking at it. In and of itself, it cannot convey meaning."[53] Yet the movement from the gate to the door is part of interpretation. This garden experience is a foil to the crowded bus ride, the colossal television screens, and the smell of octopus dumplings, which we may experience while reaching the garden entrance. The placement of stepping stones that regulate our pace, the shadows cast by the lanterns that shroud the garden in mystery, and the water basin that forces us closer to the ground to smell the fecund scent of earth and moss are part of the spiritual dimension of the ceremony.

Emotions are not only part of cognition; and some landscapes are designed specifically to elicit emotions as part of their meaning. For example, memorials—particularly ones that occupy the actual site where the event took place—can be steeped with emotional meaning. Consider the winning design proposed by Michael Arad and Peter Walker for the World Trade Tower Memorial in New York [figure 4-8]. Imagine if visitors to the memorial at the site of the former Twin Towers in New York had no emotive arousal from experiencing the memorial's garden. They simply entered the garden, read some of the names, and concluded that 2,752 people died there. In this case the garden would be a failure because it did not produce emotive responses in its visitors.

A problem arises when the intellect is privileged above emotion. Fifteen years of neuroscience suggest that emotions and rational thinking work together. According to Damasio emotions are directly tied to cognition, particularly with respect to aspects of interpretation, such as causal thinking. Based on case studies of patients he has forged a provocative theory that our decisions are weighted by emotions. Recent brain imaging studies have demonstrated that emotions actually accelerate our ability to draw conclusions and make decisions. From scientific literature to characters like Mr. Spock on *Star Trek*, twentieth-century discourse held that emotions hindered rational thought—but this research includes emotions as part of interpretation. It also suggests that the feelings and emotions evoked by gardens are important to how they mean.

CONCLUSION

Gardens can mean because designers can shape and compose their materials to express ideas and intentions to those using them. Gardens can even offer complex meanings because they are experienced with the body, and they occupy specific contexts that directly connect to their message. Interpretations of gardens by users and designers can be different. Yet, a perfect match is not always the sole aim of design, nor in other works, not even great literature. In fact, differences in interpretation can enable us to see the world anew—both for the designer and the user.

With characteristic astuteness, Treib notes that the users or "receivers" of landscapes will ultimately determine their significance.[54] Indeed, many gardens exist in a lived social context, and this social dimension of gardens is an important aspect of their ability to mean over time. Yet, the meaning of gardens interpreted by critics is important as well. Together, this intersubjective discourse identifies and forms conventions, radical breaks, basic assumptions, and ideologies. In so doing, we collectively locate the meaning of a work historically and culturally in comparison to other works of landscape architecture, art, architecture, philosophy, and literature.

Lastly, a pragmatic view of all this business about meaning suggests that—is it not better to create and cultivate gardens that can mean?

NOTES

1 Jane Gillette, "Can Gardens Mean?" *Landscape Journal*, Number 1, 2005, p. 85.

2 Ibid., p. 95.

3 Marc Treib, "Must Landscapes Mean? Approaches to Significance in Recent Landscape Architecture," *Landscape Journal*, Number 1, 1995, pp. 47–62.

4 Mark Francis and Randolph T. Hester, Jr., *The Meaning of Gardens: Idea, Place, and Action*, Cambridge, MA: MIT Press, 1990; Laurie Olin, "Form, Meaning, and Expression in Landscape Architecture," *Landscape Journal*, Number 2, 1988, pp. 149–168.

5 Arthur Danto, "The Artworld, " in Carolyn Korsmeyer, editor, *Aesthetics: The Big Questions*, London: Blackwell, 1998.

6 Gillette, "Can Gardens Mean?" p. 85.

7 John Ruskin, *Modern Painters* **III**, London: J. M. Dent, 1895.

8 Ibid., p. 151.

9 Gillette, "Can Gardens Mean?" p. 93.

10 See John Dewey, *Art and Experience*, New York: Putnam Capricorn, 1958; and Thomas M. Alexander, *John Dewey's Theory of Art, Experience, and Nature: The Horizons of Feeling*, New York: State University of New York Press, 1987.

11 Josephine Miles, *Pathetic Fallacy in the Nineteenth Century: A Study of a Changing Relation Between Object and Emotion*, New York: Octagon Books, 1965.

12 Dianne Harris, "Cultivating Power: The Language of Feminism in Women's Garden Literature, 1870–1920," *Landscape Journal*, Number 2, 1994, pp. 113–124.

13 Quoted in ibid., p. 119. See also Sophia Johnson, *Every Woman Her Own Flower Garden: A Handy Manual of Flower Gardening for Ladies*, New York: Henry T. Williams, 1874.

14 Marc Treib, editor, *Modern Landscape Architecture: A Critical Review*, Cambridge, MA: MIT Press, 1993.

15 Quoted in Reuben Rainey, "Garrett Eckbo's Landscape for Living," in Treib, *Modern Landscape Architecture*, p. 187.

16 Treib, "Must Landscapes Mean?" p. 58.

17 Ibid., p. 52.

18 Rosalind E. Krauss, *Passages in Modern Sculpture*, Cambridge, MA: MIT Press, 1989, pp. 262–263.

19 *Art On File*, ww.artonfile.com/html/ projectnotes.lasso/, accessed 5 December 2005; and Abby McCabe, "Spotlight Public Art: Building a Sense of Place and Identity," The Center for Urban and Regional Policy at Northeastern University.

20 Gillette, "Can Gardens Mean?" p. 87.

21 John Beardsley, *Earthworks and Beyond: Contemporary Art in the Landscape*, New York: Abbeville Press, 1984; Udo Weilacher, *Between Landscape Architecture and Land Art*, Basel: Birkhäuser, 1996.

22 Ibid., p. 14.

23 Beardsley, *Earthworks*, p. 7.

24 Treib, "Must Landscapes Mean?" p. 48.

25 Gillette, "Can Gardens Mean?" p. 87.

26 Larry Shiner, *The Invention of Art: A Cultural History*, Chicago: University of Chicago Press, 2001, p. 81.

27 Ibid., p. 3.

28 Gillette, "Can Gardens Mean?" p. 87.

29 Ibid., p. 88.

30 Ibid., p. 91.

31 Stephanie Ross, *What Gardens Mean*, Chicago: University of Chicago Press, 1998.

32 Ibid., pp. 179-180.

33 Gillette, "Can Gardens Mean?" p. 92.

34 Dominic McIver Lopes, *Sight and Sensibility Evaluating Pictures*, London: Oxford University Press, 2005, p. 25.

35 Gillette, "Can Gardens Mean?" p. 88.

36 Ibid.

37 Ibid., p. 91.

38 Dewey, *Art and Experience*, pp. 8–9, 10.

39 Gillette, "Can Gardens Mean?" p. 85.

40 Laurie Olin, *Across the Open Field: Essays Drawn from English Landscapes*, Philadelphia: University of Pennsylvania Press, 2000, p. 265.

41 Robert Stecker, "Interpretation," in Berys Gaut and Dominic McIver Lopes, editors, *The Routledge Companion to Aesthetics*, London: Routledge, 2002, pp. 321–334.

42 Griselda Pollock, "Modernity and the Spaces of Feminism," in Francis Francina and Jonathan Harris, editors, *Art in Modern Culture*, London: Phaidon, 1992, p. 123.

43 Michel Foucault, "What is an Author?" in Korsmeyer, *Aesthetics*, 1998.

44 Gillette, "Can Gardens Mean?" p. 88.

45 Robert Riley, "Flowers, Power and Sex," in Francis and Hester, *The Meaning of Gardens*, p. 73.

46 Matthew Potteiger and Jamie Purinton, *Landscape Narratives: Design Practices for Telling Stories*, New York: John Wiley, 1998.

47 Gillette, "Can Gardens Mean?" p. 89.

48 Ibid.

49 Ibid., p. 94.

50 Treib, "Must Landscapes Mean?" p. 60.

51 Jean Piaget, *Toward a Logic of Meanings*, Hillsdale, NJ: L. Erlbaum Associates, 1991.

52 Antonio Damasio, *The Feeling of What Happens: Body and Emotion in the Making of Consciousness*, New York: Harcourt Brace, 2000, pp. 41–42. See also Antonio Damasio, *Descartes' Error: Emotion, Reason, and the Human Brain*, New York: Putnam's Sons, 1994.

53 Gillette, "Can Gardens Mean?" p. 89.

54 Treib, "Must Landscapes Mean?" p. 60.

205 /

Commentary 4:

Meaning and Criticism

Susan Herrington

A surprising aspect of these essays is the diverse range of disciplines that the authors invoke to argue and validate their claims. In "Form, Meaning, and Expression in Landscape Architecture," Laurie Olin writes at a watershed moment when landscape architecture was finding a renewed relationship with art and history in both the profession and its academic institutions.[1] This was a time when gardens in particular were testing grounds for new ideas, and much scholarship sought to dispel the confusion between natural processes and human design. Indeed, Olin's points serve as inspirational alternatives to the burdens of McHargian landscape architecture, which condemned most art as anthropocentric, relegated historical inquiry to a fireside chat, and consistently conflated natural processes, human design, and even God.

Olin's arguments are firmly set within the humanist traditions of art history. He draws upon the methods of art historians Erwin Panofsky and Rudolf Wittkower, who sought to understand the meaning of Renaissance paintings by decoding their symbols and iconography. Dissatisfied with purely formal analyses, Panofsky and Wittkower revealed that iconography, while in plain sight, had yet to be interpreted in terms of its cultural connotations. For Panofsky, when we interpret Leonardo da Vinci's *The Last Supper* for its compositional and iconographical features as its own properties, we limit our understanding of its meaning. When we try "to understand it as a document of Leonardo's personality, or of the civilization of the Italian High Renaissance, or of a particular religious attitude, we deal with the work of art as a symptom of something else… iconography in a deeper sense."[2]

A salient dimension of this interpretive method is that it applies to the communicative properties of nonverbal arts, primarily painting and sculpture. This works well for Olin because he is concerned with how landscapes mean, but not exclusively in formal terms, and not necessarily as linguistic interpretations. To be sure, he reminds us "landscapes are not verbal constructions."[3] However, this does not preclude him from suggesting that linguistic devices can serve as design strategies. For example, he identifies metaphor as key to the process of identifying one thing as if it were something else. The idea that the symbolic content of a work—whether a painting, a landscape, or a sculpture—can communicate as a metaphor liberates the expressive content of landscapes. In turn, this expression allows landscapes to be interpreted for their meanings given by culture.

Olin admits that many features of a landscape are only as they appear. He notes, "the fact that natural materials, some of them alive, are used to represent nature and landscape (i.e., the referent and the referee may be made of the same substance) greatly complicates the matter."[4] This is an issue revisited by Gillette and later by me. For Gillette, elements in a garden "are stuck in being what they are," so they can't refer to something else.[5] I counter that the notion that art objects cannot also be real things in the world has been challenged by a century of artists and philosophers. Humans can express ideas to each other through the physical world, even with mud and stone.

While Olin is inspired by this humanist shift in landscape architecture, Marc Treib throws a cautionary light on landscape architects' newfound relationship with art and history. In "Must Landscapes Mean? Approaches to Significance in Recent Landscape Architecture" Treib responds to Olin's proposition and also the growing plethora of landscapes generated with the intent to mean.[6] He concurs with Olin's critique of McHargian landscape architecture, adding that it advances a fallacious link between analysis and design. According to Treib, "McHarg's method insinuated that if the process were correct, the form would be good, almost as if an aesthetic automatically resulted from objective study."[7] Yet he is skeptical of the alternative. Treib posits that if a scientific method authenticates McHargian landscapes, a series of semantic schools substantiates many of the works produced in the late 1980s and 1990s.[8]

Treib's analysis of these works of landscape architecture is social, if not anthropological. Much like a cultural anthropologist airlifted into a remote society with its own unwritten codes, myths, and idols, Treib demystifies the enchanting effects of these landscapes. He provides a witty classification of the ways (the Neo-archaic, the Genius of Place, the Zeitgeist, the Vernacular Landscape, the Didactic, the Theme Garden) that landscape architects have attempted to embed their work with meaning. The first four are heavily in debt to history to assert meaning. For example, students of the Neo-archaic School use rocks, sacred groves, and spiral paths as vague gestures to the past—a past so far away in time it eclipses style, but, as Treib reveals, creates its own identifiable belief system.

These classifications are refreshing because they expose seemingly diverse and original landscapes as socially constructed, reproduced, and a bit predictable. Moreover, in our rush to design landscapes that communicate, Treib questions if people have the knowledge to interpret them. For Treib any symbolic system requires education, but he reminds us that meaning can also be sensually induced.[9] According to Treib an emphasis on pleasure and the senses is absent from many recent landscapes, but it is also absent from Treib's own analysis. It would have been interesting to assess the discussed landscapes based on their sensuous pleasure, for we may in fact find another set of classifications.

Treib makes an important distinction between landscape meaning and significance. Significance, he asserts, accrues with time and is assigned by the users not necessarily the designers. He does not delve into the actual machinery of how and if landscapes can communicate. This angle is addressed by Jane Gillette. She not only agrees that knowledge is key to interpretation but wonders if gardens can communicate at all, or even if one would want to interpret them. In "Can Gardens Mean?" Gillette makes the astute point that this discourse on landscape and garden meaning has assumed all along that gardens can mean.

Building upon Treib's argument that the strength of a garden lies in its ability to provide beauty and delight, Gillette questions if this might hinder a garden's ability to communicate any cognitive messages. "How many of us have walked through a perfectly beautiful landscape by Andropogon, and never suspected that something meaningful was afoot? This unconsciousness is part of Andropogon's design intent."[10] Meaning in "Can Gardens Mean?" is cognitive consciousness and its contrary is unconsciousness or subconscious pleasure, which is perceived as not meaning.

Gillette's argument shares aspects of Clement Greenberg's formalism, which shuns representational and illusionistic appreciations of art, and values art for the way its form expresses its medium. For example, painting is valuable for its expression as paint on a flat canvas, not for what it is trying to represent—a picnic lunch in a Parisian park, perhaps. Furthermore, valuing various arts is predicated upon distinguishing what their inherent methods and materials afford. Thus, "each art had to define itself in terms of the limitations of its proper medium."[11] Gillette turns this theory to gardens stating that there is "no subject, no area of significance, that could only be expressed by the garden. Behind this observation lies my critical assumption that every medium champions itself; so that if people make gardens to express ideas, we need to ask what ideas require the garden for its full and best expression that cannot be adequately achieved by some other medium." She identifies garden elements as "water in the form of lakes, rivers, and fountains; paving of all sorts; walls, benches, statuary; grading; follies that range from grottos to temples; and flower, trees, stones, and shrubs" as part of the material inherent to garden design.[12]

Certainly, once we unpack the line *can gardens mean* as the possible, likely, or even appropriate ability to mean, we can quickly pick out situations where the conveyance of meaning is best suited for the written word over these elements—lease agreements, grocery lists, or driver manuals. Even the written words that accompany the elaborate drawings produced by professional landscapes architects are taken for legal fact over the design's depiction in drawing form. Yes, words are useful, powerful, and can be poetic, but there are expressions, such as tranquility or the sublime, that might be better communicated through an experience with a garden than a text. Or perhaps not, it really depends on the art of the text and the garden, and the person experiencing them. Also, words are not always a direct expression of what they literally say. The philosopher Robert Stecker notes that the utterance, "there are ten sheep in the field," could mean that we are missing two sheep from our herd of twelve sheep.[13]

The gist of my response in "Gardens Can Mean" asks why must meaning be only optically understood and cognitive in its message and interpretation, and why must we adhere to formalism since the past quarter-century has challenged the validity of this theory?[14] Here, I propose an account of meaning as a verb, which is different from the adjective, meaningful (although, I think all four authors tend to blur the verb to mean with the adjectives, meaningful or significant). Since I am concerned with the ability of landscapes and gardens to mean, I offer a version of meaning that takes into account interpretation. In order to determine if gardens can mean, interpretation must be considered. According to Stecker, when we interpret we are "attempting to discover or, at least, ascribe on some basis, a meaning in or to the work in question, or to determine what significance the work has for us."[15] My understanding of meaning and the way it is interpreted includes multiple interpretations, movement, sensations, and emotions. Since many landscapes are spaces that we move through and experience viscerally, these other dimensions are important for expressing ideas to others.

My critique in "Gardens Can Mean" is influenced by John Dewey's pragmatism.[16] Dewey thought that art should contribute meaning in everyday life and not be locked up in a museum. He also claimed aesthetic experiences were social in nature, not internal dialogues with the self. Given that gardens and landscapes feature frequently in people's daily lives and the fact that they are often social spaces, this makes them ideal locations for meaning. Since many gardens and landscapes are public they are also open to diverse interpretations by designers, users, and critics.

An uncertainty that lingers in all four essays is: to what extent does the designer's intent play in the role of critical interpretation? This is a frequent question in aesthetics and art criticism. The philosopher Noel Carroll states that "there is probably no more disputed issue concerning interpretation than the question of what role if any the intention of the artist should play in criticism."[17] Carroll argues that "the artist's intentions are relevant to the evaluation of artworks inasmuch as the critic needs to take on what the artist intended in order to determine what, precisely, the artist has done.[18] For Carroll, the critic does not evaluate the designer's intention; instead, in grasping what the designer has achieved she will depend on some knowledge of the designer's intentions. This does not limit the meaning of landscapes. Returning to the meadow at Avalon Park, Andropogon's designers did not intend the meadow to communicate any ideas. However, this does not stop the local ecologist, who has been studying plant life in the meadow for ten years, from gleaning loads of cognitive content from the meadow. Ultimately, we can learn quite a bit about the human imagination and landscapes by considering the diverse interpretations that they portend. These interpretations can forge new ways of seeing landscapes. For example, J. B. Jackson's interpretations of the everyday landscape of garages, small town streetscapes, and mobile-home courts instigated a critical subfield in landscape architecture—the study of vernacular landscapes.

In "Gardens Can Mean" I also expand the cognitive definition of meaning. Gillette supports the sensorial and pleasure-based value of gardens but it is presented in opposition to meaning. I propose that sensory impressions and feelings are part of meaning and to some extent I think Olin agrees with this position. I point to research by neuroscientists who have demonstrated that our brains are not locked in a bottle and that our body, sensory experiences, and emotions are directly connected to cognition and even rational thinking.

While landscape architecture lies at the margins of art, the arguments elaborated by the four authors reflect central debates in art history, art criticism, anthropology, and philosophy. As such, the debate over landscape and meaning cannot be subjected to methodological reductionism. Landscape criticism is an unfolding enterprise, involving evaluations and propositions based on difference. Moreover, our differences tell us something about landscape architecture itself. We know that landscape architecture does not develop independently of particular historical moments, but the various claims made by these authors over the past twenty years also suggest that it does not evolve independently of criticism either.

Notes

1 Laurie Olin, "Form, Meaning, and Expression in Landscape Architecture," *Landscape Journal*, Number 2, 1988, pp. 149–168.

2 Erwin Panofsky, *Studies in Iconology: Humanist Themes in the Art of the Renaissance*, New York: Harper & Row, 1972, p. 8.

3 Olin, "Form, Meaning, and Expression," p. 158.

4 Ibid., p. 165.

5 Jane Gillette, "Can Gardens Mean?" *Landscape Journal*, Number 1, 2005, p. 91.

6 Marc Treib, "Must Landscapes Mean? Approaches to Significance in Recent Landscape Architecture, *Landscape Journal*, Number 1, 1995, pp. 47–62.

7 Ibid., p. 49.

8 Ibid., p. 50.

9 Ibid., pp. 55, 59.

10 Gillette, "Can Gardens Mean?" p. 88.

11 Charles Harrison and Paul Wood, editors, Preface to "The American Avant-Garde: Clement Greenburg 'Towards a Newer Laocoön,'" in *Art Theory 1900–1990: An Anthology of Changing Ideas*, Malden, MA: Blackwell, 2000, p. 554.

12 Gillette, "Can Gardens Mean?" p. 87.

13 Robert Stecker, "Interpretation," in Berys Gaut and Dominic McIver Lopes, editors, *The Routledge Companion to Aesthetics*, London: Routledge, 2002, p. 328.

14 Susan Herrington, "Gardens Can Mean," *Landscape Journal*, Number 2, 2007, pp. 302–317.

15 Stecker, "Interpretation," p. 321.

16 Susan Herrington, "When Art is a Garden: Benny Farm by Claude Cormier," in Michel Conan, editor, *Contemporary Garden Aesthetics, Creations and Interpretations*, Washington, D.C.: Dumbarton Oaks, 2007, pp. 17–32; and John Dewey, *Art and Experience*, New York: Putnam Capricorn, 1958.

17 Noel Carroll, *On Criticism*, New York: Routledge, 2009, p. 134.

18 Ibid., p. 81.

BIBLIOGRAPHY

Adams, Howard, and Stewart Wrede, editors. *Denatured Visions.* New York: Museum of Modern Art, 1991.

Alexander, Thomas M. *John Dewey's Theory of Art, Experience, and Nature: The Horizons of Feeling.* New York: State University of New York Press, 1987.

Barthes, Roland. *The Pleasure of the Text.* Richard Miller, trans. New York: Hill and Wang, 1975.

Beardsley, John. *Earthworks and Beyond: Contemporary Art in the Landscape.* New York: Abbeville Press, 1984.

Bellman, David. "Frederick Law Olmsted and a Plan for Mount Royal Park." In *Mount Royal, Montreal, Supplement #1, Canadian Art Revue.* Ottawa, Canada, 1977, pp. 53–57.

Brown, Brenda, editor. "Eco-Revelatory Design: Nature Constructed/ Nature Revealed," *Landscape Journal,* Special Issue 1998.

Burke, Edmund. *A Philosophical Enquiry into the Origin of Our Ideas of the Sublime and Beautiful.* James T. Boulton, editor. Notre Dame: University of Notre Dame Press, 1968.

Calasso, Roberto. *Ka: Stories of the Mind and Gods of India.* New York: A. A. Knopf, 1998.

Coffin, David, editor. *The Italian Garden.* Washington, D.C.: Dumbarton Oaks, 1972.

———. *The Villa in the Life of Renaissance Rome.* Princeton, NJ: Princeton University Press, 1979.

Colquhoun, Alan. "Form and Figure," *Oppositions 12,* Spring 1978, pp. 29–37.

Damasio, Antonio. *Descartes' Error: Emotion, Reason, and the Human Brain*. New York: Putnam's Sons, 1994.

———. *The Feeling of What Happens: Body and Emotion in the Making of Consciousness*. New York: Harcourt Brace, 2000.

Danto, Arthur. "The Artworld." In *Aesthetics: The Big Questions*, Carolyn Korsmeyer, editor. London: Blackwell, 1998.

———. *Transformation of the Commonplace*. Cambridge, MA: Harvard University Press, 1981.

Dewey, John. *Art and Experience*. New York: Putnam Capricorn, 1958.

Dwyer, Gary. "The Power under Our Feet." *Landscape Architecture*, May–June, 1986, pp. 65–68.

Eckbo, Garrett. *Landscapes for Living*. New York: Reinhold Publishing, 1950.

Evenson, Norma. *Paris: A Century of Change*. New Haven, CT: Yale University Press, 1978.

Fish, Margery. *We Made a Garden*. New York: Modern Library, 2002.

Foucault, Michel. "What Is an Author?" In *Aesthetics: The Big Questions*, Carolyn Korsmeyer, editor. London: Blackwell, 1998.

Francis, Mark, and Randolph T. Hester, Jr., editors. *The Meaning of Gardens*. Cambridge, MA: MIT Press, 1989.

Garreau, Edward. *Edge City*. Garden City, NY: Doubleday, 1991.

Gideon, Sigfried. *Space, Time and Architecture*. Cambridge, MA: Harvard University Press, 1938.

Gillette, Jane. "Can Gardens Mean?" *Landscape Journal*, Number 1, 2005, pp. 85–97.

Glacken, Clarence J. *Traces on the Rhodian Shore: Nature and Culture in Western Thought from Ancient Times to the End of the Eighteenth Century.* Berkeley: University of California Press, 1967.

Goethe, J. W. von. "The Collector and His Circle." *Propyläen II*, 1799. In *Goethe on Art*, John Gage, editor. Berkeley: University of California Press, 1980.

Goodman, Nelson. *Ways of Worldmaking.* Cambridge, MA: Hackett Publishing Company, 1978.

Greenberg, Clement. "American Type Painting." In *Art and Culture: Critical Essays.* Boston: Beacon Press, 1961.

Harris, Dianne. "Cultivating Power: The Language of Feminism in Women's Garden Literature, 1870–1920." *Landscape Journal*, Number 2, 1994, pp. 113–124.

Hayakawa, Masao. *The Garden Art of Japan.* Tokyo: Heibonsha, 1973.

Herrington, Susan. "Landscapes Can Mean." *Landscape Journal*, Number 2, 2007, pp. 302–317.

Hoskins, W. H. *The Making of the English Landscape.* Harmondsworth: Penguin Books, 1955.

Hunt, John Dixon. "Stourhead Revisited & the Pursuit of Meaning in Gardens." *Studies in the History of Gardens and Designed Landscapes*, October–December 2006, pp. 328–341.

—— "The Garden as Cultural Object." In *Denatured Visions*, Howard Adams and Stewart Wrede, editors. New York: Museum of Modern Art, 1991.

——. *Greater Perfections: The Practice of Garden Theory.* Philadelphia: University of Pennsylvania Press, 2000.

Husserl, Edmund. *Logical Investigations*. J. N. Findlay, translator. New York: Humanities Press, 1970.

Jackson, John Brinckerhoff. *The Necessity for Ruins*. Amherst, MA: University of Massachusetts Press, 1980.

———. *Landscapes*. Amherst, MA: University of Massachusetts Press, 1970.

———. *Defining the Vernacular Landscape*. New Haven, UK: Yale University Press, 1984.

Jellicoe, Geoffrey. *Landscapes of Civilization*. Woodbridge, CT: Garden Art Press, 1989.

Johnson, Sophia. *Every Woman Her Own Flower Garden. A Handy Manual of Flower Gardening for Ladies*. New York: Henry T. Williams, 1874.

Kelsall, Malcolm. "The Iconography of Stourhead." *Journal of the Warburg and Courtauld Institutes*, 1983, pp. 133–143.

Knight, Richard Payne. *An Analytical Inquiry into the Principles of Taste*. London, 1805.

Korsmeyer, Carolyn, editor. *Aesthetics: The Big Questions*. London: Blackwell, 1998.

Krauss, Rosalind E. *Passages in Modern Sculpture*. Cambridge, MA: MIT Press, 1989.

Krog, Steven. "Creative Risk Taking." *Landscape Architecture*, March 1983, pp. 70–76.

———. "Is it Art?" *Landscape Architecture*, May 1981, pp. 373–376.

Kuhn, Thomas S. *The Structure of Scientific Revolutions*. Chicago: University of Chicago Press, 1964.

Lippard, Lucy. *Overlays*. New York: E. P. Dutton & Co, 1983.

Lopes, Dominic McIver. *Sight and Sensibility: Evaluating Pictures*. London: Oxford University Press, 2005.

MacDougall, Elisabeth. *"Ars Hortulorum*: Sixteenth-Century Garden Iconography and Literary Theory in Italy." In *The Italian Garden*, David Coffin, editor. Washington, D.C.: Dumbarton Oaks, 1972.

Martin, Alex, and Jerome Fletcher. *The Decadent Gardener*. Sawtry, U.K.: Daedalus, 1996.

McHarg, Ian. *Design with Nature*. Garden City, NY: Doubleday, 1969.

Meinig, D. W., editor. *The Interpretation of Ordinary Landscapes*. New York: Oxford University Press, 1979.

Miles, Josephine. *Pathetic Fallacy in the Nineteenth Century: A Study of a Changing Relation between Object and Emotion*. New York: Octagon Books, 1965.

Miller, Mara. *The Garden as Art*. Albany, NY: State University of New York Press, 1993.

Mohanty, J. N. "Husserl's Theory of Meaning." In *Husserl Expositions and Appraisals*, Frederick Elliston and Peter McCormick, editors. South Bend, IN: University of Notre Dame Press, 1977.

Neckar, Lance. "Castle Howard: An Original Landscape Architecture." *Landscape Journal*, Number 1, 2000, pp. 20–45.

Norberg-Schulz, Christian. *Genius Loci*. New York: Rizzoli, 1980.

Ogden, C. K., and I. A. Richards. *The Meaning of Meaning*. New York: Harcourt, Brace & World, 1923.

Olin, Laurie. "Form, Meaning, and Expression in Landscape Architecture." *Landscape Journal*, Number 2, 1988, 149–168.

——. *Across the Open Field: Essays Drawn from English Landscapes.* Philadelphia: University of Pennsylvania Press, 2000.

Olmsted, Frederick Law. "Montreal: A Mountain Top Park and Some Thoughts on Art and Nature." In *Civilizing American Cities*, S. B. Sutton, editor. Cambridge, MA: MIT Press, 1971.

Pollock, Griselda. "Modernity and the Spaces of Feminism." In *Art in Modern Culture*, Francis Francina and Jonathan Harris, editors. London: Phaidon, 1992.

Potteiger, Matthew, and Jamie Purinton. *Landscape Narratives: Design Practices for Telling Stories.* New York: John Wiley, 1998.

Price, Uvedale. *An Essay on the Picturesque.* London, 1794.

Rainey, Reuben. "'Organic Form in the Humanized Landscape': Garrett Eckbo's *Landscape for Living*." In *Modern Landscape Architecture: A Critical Review*, Marc Treib, editor. Cambridge, MA: MIT Press, 1993.

Relph, Edward. *Place and Placelessness.* London: Pion Limited, 1976.

Riley, Robert B. "From Sacred Grove to Disney World: The Search for Garden Meaning." *Landscape Journal*, Number 2, 1988.

Rodgers, Elizabeth Barlow. *Landscape Design: A Cultural and Architectural History.* New York: Harry N. Abrams, 2001.

Ross, Stephanie. *What Gardens Mean.* Chicago: University of Chicago Press, 1998.

Ruskin, John. *Modern Painters III.* London: J. M. Dent, 1895.

Schwartz, Martha. "Landscape and Common Culture." In *Modern Landscape Architecture*, Marc Treib, editor. Cambridge, MA: MIT Press, 1993.

Shiner, Larry. *The Invention of Art: A Cultural History*. Chicago: University of Chicago Press, 2001.

Spirn, Anne Whiston. *The Language of Landscape*. New Haven CT: Yale University Press, 1998.

Stecker, Robert. "Interpretation." In *The Routledge Companion to Aesthetics*, Berys Gaut and Dominic McIver Lopes, editors. London: Routledge, 2002.

Steenbergen, Clemens, and Wouter Reh with Gerrit Smienk. "The Magic of the Formal." In *Architecture and Landscape: the Design Experiment of Great European Gardens and Landscapes*. New York: Prestel, 1996.

Takei, Jiro, and Marc P. Keane, translators. *Sakuteiki: Visions of the Japanese Garden: A Modern Translation of Japan's Gardening Classic*. Boston: Tuttle Publishing, 2001.

Treib, Marc. "Axioms for a Modern Landscape Architecture." In *Modern Landscape Architecture, A Critical Review*, Marc Treib, editor. Cambridge, MA: MIT Press, 1993.

——. "Must Landscapes Mean? Approaches to Significance in Recent Landscape Architecture." *Landscape Journal*, Number 1, 1995, pp. 47–62.

——. "Traces upon the Land: The Formalistic Landscape," *Architectural Association Quarterly*, Number 4, 1979. Reprinted in Marc Treib, *Settings and Stray Paths: Writings on Landscapes and Gardens*. London: Routledge, 2005.

Tunnard, Christopher. *Gardens in the Modern Landscape*. London: Architectural Press, 1938.

Williamson, Tom. *Polite Landscapes: Gardens and Society in Eighteenth-Century England*. Baltimore: Johns Hopkins University Press, 1995.

Wittkower, Rudolph. "Classical Theory and Eighteenth-Century Sensibility." In *Palladio and English Palladianism*. New York: Thames and Hudson, 1966.

Zevi, Bruno. *Architecture as Space*. New York: Horizon Press, 1957.

Art On File. www.artonfile.com/html/projectnotes.lasso/ (accessed December 5, 2005).

McCabe, Abby. "Spotlight Public Art: Building a Sense of Place and Identity." The Center for Urban and Regional Policy at Northeastern University. http://www.curp.neu.edu/sitearchive/spotlight.asp?id=2166/ (accessed December 5, 2005).

CONTRIBUTORS

Jane Gillette is a writer who has served as features editor of *Landscape Architecture* magazine, associate editor of *Historic Preservation* magazine, editor of the journal *Land Forum*, and managing editor of the Spacemaker Press.

Susan Herrington is Associate Professor of Architecture and Landscape Architecture at the University of British Columbia. Her writings have spanned a variety of subjects that include theoretical subjects as well as the landscapes of play. *On Landscape* appeared in 2009.

Laurie Olin is a founding member of the OLIN Studio and Professor in Practice at the University of Pennsylvania whose appointments include chair of the Harvard University Department of Landscape Architecture. *Across the Open Field: Essays Drawn from the English Landscape*, published in 2000, remains one of the most insightful views on the subject.

Marc Treib is Professor of Architecture Emeritus at the University of California, Berkeley; he has written, edited, and designed books on landscape architecture, design, and architecture, on both historical and contemporary subjects.

INDEX

Aeneid, The (Virgil), 158, 161, 169

Afterlife of Gardens, The
(John Dixon Hunt), 79

Alphand, Adolphe, 27

*Analytic Inquiry into the Principles of
Taste, An* (Richard Payne Knight), 150

Andre, Carl, 31, 94, 181; *Stone Field
Sculpture*, 94, 181

André, Édouard, 66

Andropogon Associates, 143, 195–196,
209, 211; Avalon Park, New York,
196, 211

Arad, Michael, 201; World Trade
Center Memorial (with Peter Walker),
New York, 201

Aristotle, 56–57, 171

Arp, Jean (Hans), 86

Asplund, Gunnar, Woodland
Cemetery (with Sigurd Lewerentz),
Enskede, Sweden, 111–112

Austen, Jane, 148

Aycock, Alice, 32

Baird, George viii; *Meaning in Architecture* (with Charles Jencks), viii

Barthes, Roland, 115, 116

Bauhaus, 188

Beardsley, John, 182, 184; *Earthworks
and Beyond*, 182

Beethoven, Ludwig van, 76

Benjamin, Walter, 188

Bernini, Gianlorenzo, 28

Between Landscape and Land Art
(Udo Weilacher), 182, 184

Bridgeman, Charles, 36

Brown, Lancelot "Capability," 36, 40,
52, 56; Blenheim, England, 41

Burke, Edmund, 150; *Philosophical
Inquiry into the Origin and Ideas of the
Sublime and Beautiful*, 150

Bye, A. E., 60, 64; Soros garden,
New York, 60

Cage, John, xvii

Calvino, Italo, 169

Carroll, Noel, 211

Carson, Rachel, 127

Central Park (Frederick Law Olmsted
and Calvert Vaux), New York, 51, 52,
54, 55

Chemetoff, Alexandre, 101, 184;
Bamboo Garden, Parc de la Villette,
Paris, 101, 184

Chernikov, Iakov, 129

Child's Christmas in Wales, A
(Dylan Thomas), ix

Church, Thomas, 60, 86

Clément, Gilles, 104; Parc André
Citroën, Paris, 104

Colquhoun, Alan, xii, 43, 45, 58

Cormier, Claude, 184, 186;
Place d'Youville, Montreal, 186

Da Vinci, Leonardo, 207

Dalí, Salvador, 30

Damasio, Antonio, 200, 201

Danadjieva, Angela, 64

Danto, Arthur, 35, 50, 59, 176, 190;
Transformation of the Commonplace, 59

David, Enrico, xv

223 /

De Chirico, Giorgio, 30, 33

De Hooch, Pieter, 30

De Saussure, Ferdinand, 130

Design with Nature (Ian McHarg), x, 87, 127

Dewey, John, 190, 193, 211

Duchamp, Marcel, 36, 190

Dumbarton Oaks, Washington, D.C., 44

Dwyer, Gary, 89–90

Eames, Charles, 116

earthworks (land art), 73, 177, 182, 184, 188

Earthworks and Beyond (John Beardsley), 182

Eckbo, Garrett, 27, 66, 85, 86, 87, 129, 180; *Landscape for Living,* 87, 180

Edge City (Joel Garreau), 100

Eisenman, Peter, 58; Memorial to the Murdered Jews of Europe, Berlin, 80

Evenson, Norma, 96

Essay on the Picturesque, An (Uvedale Price), 150

Finlay, Ian Hamilton, 80, 162, 182; Little Sparta (Stony Path), 80, 162

Fish, Margery, 138

Folk Housing in Middle Virginia (Henry Glassie), ix

Foucault, Michel, 195

Frampton, Kenneth, 58

Francis, Mark, x, 84, 174; *The Meaning of Gardens* (with Randolph T. Hester, Jr.), x, 84, 174, 197

Frost, Robert, 196

Fuller, Buckminster, 25

Furness, Frank, 55

gardens, French,36, 38, 40, 41, 110; Italian, 44, 48, 49, 50, 64; Japanese, xiv, 44, 56, 106, 108, 143, 144, 169–170, 190, 192

Garreau, Joel, 100; *Edge City,* 100

Gehry, Frank, 31, 98

Gideon, Sigfried, 86

Gillette, Jane, xiii, xvii, 75, 174, 176, 178, 179, 180, 188, 194, 196, 197, 198, 200, 207, 209, 212

Glacken, Clarence, 139, 140; *Traces on the Rhodian Shore,* 139

Glassie, Henry, ix; *Folk Housing in Middle Virginia,* ix

Glen, Robert, 28

Goethe, J. W. von, 117

Goodman, Nelson, 44, 50, 75–76, 77, 128; *Ways of Worldmaking,* 44

Graves, Michael, 33

Greater Perfections (John Dixon Hunt), 79, 137

Greenberg, Clement, 59, 86–87, 209

Guevrekian, Gabriel, 27, 66; *Garden of Water and Light,* 27

Haag, Richard, 60, 61–62, 64, 69; Bloedel Reserve, Washington, 61–62, 69; Gasworks Park, Seattle, 61, 69

Halprin, Lawrence, 60, 62, 64, 80; Auditorium Forecourt Fountain, Portland, 64; Roosevelt Memorial, Washington, D.C., 80

Hargreaves, George, 25, 28, 30, 66, 89, 146, 195; Harlequin Plaza, Denver, Colorado, 25, 32, 33, 89

Hargreaves Associates, 128

Harries, Mags, 182

Harris, Dianne, 179

Hazlehurst, Hamilton, 58

Hegel, Georg Wilhelm Friedrich, 44

Heizer, Michael, 32

Herrington, Susan, xiii, xiv, xviii, 127, 170

Hester, Randolph T., Jr., x, 84, 174; *The Meaning of Gardens* (with Mark Francis), x, 84, 174, 197

Hiorns, Roger, xv

Hoare, Henry II, xiii, 56, 139, 156, 194, 195

Hollis, Douglas, 101; *A Sound Garden*, 101

Holt, Nancy, 32

Howett, Catherine, 90

Hunt, John Dixon, 78–79, 108, 110, 137, 151; *The Afterlife of Gardens*, 79; *Greater Perfections*, 137

Husserl, Edmund, 44

Innes, Georges, 36

Irwin, Robert, 27

Japan, xiv, 202; gardens, xiv, 44, 56, 143, 144, 169–170, 190, 192

Jencks, Charles, viii; *Meaning in Architecture* (with George Baird), viii

Jensen, Jens, 52

Johnson, Sophia, 179, *My Flowers*, 179

Joyce, James, xvii

Kandinsky, Wassily, 129

Kant, Immanuel, 36

Katsura Villa, Kyoto, 44, 108

Kent, William, 36, 56

Kiley, Dan, 60, 64

Klein, Yves, xvi

Knight, Richard Payne, 150; *An Analytic Inquiry into the Principles of Taste*, 150

Koch, Kenneth, 58

Krauss, Rosalind, 181

Krog, Steven, 73

landscape: actuality, 167–169 passim.; as medium, 188, 189, 190, 209–210; eco-revelatory, 146; form, 25, 34–35; design intentions in, 140, 190, 194, 196, 208, 209; interpretation of, 192, 195, 196, 197, 199, 200, 207, 202, 209, 210–212; materials, 26–27; metaphor, 56–59, 207; narrative, 168, 177, 181, 186, 197; pleasure and/or comfort in, 115, 116, 132, 167, 181, 182, 186, 207, 212; representation of, 167, 168; sensual experience of, 117, 200, 208, 209, 212

Landscape Journal, xi, xii, 75, 176, 127

Landscape for Living (Garrett Eckbo), 87, 180

Landscape Narratives (Matthew Potteiger and Jamie Purinton), 151, 197–198

Langer, Suzanne, 190

language, 194, 197, 198, 207

Language of Landscape, The
(Anne Whiston Spirn), 198

Le Nôtre, André, 36, 40, 41; Chantilly, 38; Vaux le Vicomte, 38, 41; Sceaux, 38; Versailles, 38, 41, 110

Leader, Darian, xv

Lenné, Peter Joseph, 27

Lewerentz, Sigurd, Woodland Cemetery (with Gunnar Asplund), Enskede, Sweden, 111–112

Long, Richard, 89, 94

Lopes, Dominic, 192

Lorrain, Claude, 36

Louis XIV, 110

Manet, Édouard, 195; *Olympia*, 195; *A Bar at the Folies-Bergère*, 195

McAvin, Margaret, xii

McHarg, Ian, x, 87–88, 127, 206, 208; *Design with Nature*, x, 87, 127

Meaning of Gardens, The (Mark Francis and Randolph T. Hester, Jr., editors), 84, 174, 197

Meaning of Meaning, The (C. K. Ogden and I. A Richards), 128

memorials, 202

memory, 199

Mendieta, Ana, 89

Merleau-Ponty, Maurice, 90

Metamorphoses, The (Ovid), 49, 158, 161

minimalist art, 181

Miss, Mary, 32, 182

Mock, Dan, 25

Modern Landscape Architecture: A Critical Review (Marc Treib, editor), 180

Modern Painters III (John Ruskin), 177–178

Morris, William, 54

Muir, John, 48

"My Flowers" (Sophia Johnson), 179

national parks, 49

Nicholson, Harold, 129; Sissinghurst (with Vita Sackville-West), England, 129

Noguchi, Isamu, 86, 89, 180–181; *California Scenario*, Costa Mesa, California, 180–181

Norberg-Schulz, Christian, 90

Ogden, C. K., 128; *The Meaning of Meaning* (with I. A. Richards), 128

Olin, Laurie, xi, xii, xvii, xviii, 84, 87, 127, 148, 156, 158, 160, 161, 168, 174, 194, 199, 206, 207, 208, 212; Memorial to the Murdered Jews of Europe, Berlin (with Peter Eisenman), 80

Olmsted, Frederick Law, 27, 48, 52, 66, 79; Central Park (with Calvert Vaux), New York, 51, 52, 54, 55; Prospect Park, New York, 52, 55

Ovid, 49, 158; *Metamorphoses, The,* 49, 158, 161

Palladio, Andrea, 38

Panofsky, Erwin, 50, 206, 207

Parc André Citroën (Gilles Clément et al.), Paris, 104

Parc de la Villette (Bernard Tschumi), Paris, 96, 98, 141

pathetic fallacy, 138, 167, 177–180

Patio of the Oranges, Seville, 91

Paxton, Joseph, 27

Philosophical Inquiry into the Origin and Ideas of the Sublime and Beautiful, A (Edmund Burke), 150

Piaget, Jean, 200

Piper, Fredrik Magnus, 102, 129; Drottningholm, 129; Haga Park, Stockholm, 102, 129

Plato, 171

Pollock, Griselda, 195

Pope, Alexander, 90, 128

Popper, Karl, 44

post-structuralism, 197

postmodernism, 141

Potteiger, Matthew, 151, 154, 162, 198, *Landscape Narratives* (with Jamie Purinton), 151, 197–198

Price, Uvedale, 150; *An Essay on the Picturesque*, 150

Proust, Marcel, 151

Pugin, Augustus Welby Northmore, 52

Purinton, Jamie, 151, 154, 162, 198; *Landscape Narratives* (with Matthew Potteiger), 151, 197–198

Repton, Humphry, 56

Reeves, Jim, 25

Richards, I. A., 128; *The Meaning of Meaning* (with C. K. Ogden), 128

Riley, Robert, xii, 84, 127

Rose, James, 84, 85, 86, 87, 127, 197

Ross, Stephanie, 160, 190; *What Gardens Mean*, 160–161, 190

Rossi, Aldo, 33

Rousham Hall, England, 50, 110

Ruskin, John, 52, 54, 177–178, *Modern Painters III*, 177–178

Ryoan-ji, Kyoto, Japan, xiv, 44, 169, 170, 190, 192, 193

Sackville-West, Vita, 129; Sissinghurst, England (with Harold Nicholson), 129

Schwartz, Martha, 25, 26, 27, 31, 32, 66, 88, 98, 129, 145, 152, 154, 184; Bagel Garden, 25, 26; Rio Shopping Center, 152, 154, 162; Splice Garden, 145–46

Sherman, Cindy, 190

Shiner, Larry, 188

Silvetti, Jorge, 58

Sissinghurst, England (Vita Sackville-West and Harold Nicholson), 104, 129

Skaer, Lucy, xv

Smith, Ken, 184

Smithson, 89, 128, 182, *Spiral Hill*, 128

Spirn, Anne Whiston, xi, 127, 144, 150, 162, 193, 198; *The Language of Landscape*, 198

Star Trek, 203

Stebbins, Emma, 51; Bethesda Fountain, Central Park, New York, 51

Stecker, Robert, 210, 211

Steele, Fletcher, 66, 102; Naumkeag, Massachusetts, 102

Stein, Gertrude, xvii

Stourhead, England, xiii, 50, 51, 75, 139, 156, 158, 160, 161, 162, 169, 176, 194–195, 199

Stowe, England, 50

Sullivan, Louis, 55

sustainability, 130

Suzuki, Daisetz, xvii

SWA (Jim Reeves, Dan Mock), 25, 28, 33; Williams Square, 25, 28, 33

Swaffield, Simon, 74; *Theory in Landscape Architecture*, 74

Tale of Genji (Lady Murasaki), 115

Thomas, Dylan, ix; *A Child's Christmas in Wales*, ix

Thoreau, Henry David, 48

Traces on the Rhodian Shore (Clarence Glacken), 139

Transformation of the Commonplace (Arthur Danto), 59

Treib, Marc, 74, 134, 140, 141, 149, 166, 174, 176, 180, 181, 199, 203, 208, 209; *Modern Landscape Architecture: A Critical Review*, 180

Tschumi, Bernard, 96, 98, 129; Parc de la Villette, Paris, 96, 98, 129

Tunnard, Christopher, 85, 87

Van der Rohe, Ludwig Mies, 129; German Pavilion, Barcelona, 129

Van Valkenburg, Michael, 66

Vanvitelli, Luigi, 28

Vaux, Calvert, 52, 54

Venturi, Robert, 58, 98

Versailles, France (André Le Nôtre), 38, 41, 162

Vidler, Anthony, 58

Virgil, 158, 194–195, 196; *The Aeneid*, 158, 161, 169

Vitruvius, 117

Vogt, Gunther, 129; *Garden of Violence*, 129

Walker, Emmett, 151

Walker, Peter, 26, 27, 31, 66, 94, 181, 202; IBM Solana, Texas, 94; Tanner Fountain, 26, 94, 181, 182; World Trade Center Memorial (with Michael Arad), 202

Warhol, Andy, 188

Ways of Worldmaking (Nelson Goodman), 44

Weilacher, Udo, 184; *Between Landscape and Land Art*, 182, 184

Weintraub, Lee, 66

What Gardens Mean (Stephanie Ross), 160–161, 190

Wise, Henry, 36

Wittkower, Rudolf, 50, 206, 207

Wollheim, Richard, 190

Woodbridge, Kenneth, 58

Woodland Cemetery (Gunnar Asplund and Sigurd Lewerentz), Enskede, Sweden, 111–112

Wordsworth, Dorothy and William, 178

Wright, Frank Lloyd, 79

Wright, Richard, xvi

Wyeth, Andrew, 34

All rights reserved. No part of this book may be reprinted or reproduced or utilized in any form or by any electronic, mechanical, or other means, now known or hereafter invented, including photocopying and recording, or in any information storage or retrieval system, without permission in writing from the publishers.

The authors and publishers gratefully acknowledge those who have given permission to reproduce material in this book. Every effort has been made to contact copyright holders for the permission to reprint material in this book. The publishers would be grateful to hear from any copyright holder who is not acknowledged here and will undertake to rectify any errors or omissions in future editions of the book

Laurie Olin, "Form, Meaning, and Expression in Landscape Architecture," was originally published in *Landscape Journal* 7.2 (1989).
© 1988 Board of Regents of the University of Wisconsin System.

Marc Treib, "Must Landscapes Mean? Approaches to Significance in Recent Landscape Architecture," was originally published in *Landscape Journal* 14.1. (1995).
© 1995 Board of Regents of the University of Wisconsin System.

Jane Gillette, "Can Gardens Mean?" was originally published in *Landscape Journal* 24.1 (2005).
© 2005 Board of Regents of the University of Wisconsin System.

Susan Herrington, "Gardens Can Mean," was originally published in *Landscape Journal* 26.2 (2007).
© 2005 Board of Regents of the University of Wisconsin System.